The Total Writing Program

Get Writing!!

Book 2 Grades 2-3
Paragraphs and Forms of Writing

Leif Fearn and Nancy Farnan

ecs

This book is dedicated to the teachers who worked with us over the years, refining our profession's understanding of how to teach children and adolescents to write well. We particularly appreciate Suzanne Jackson, Ellen Phaneuf, and Diane Rocha.

These popular teacher resources and activity books are available from
ECS Learning Systems, Inc. for Grades Pre-K–6

AlphaCapers and Characters	Gr. Pre-K-1	2 Titles
Booklinks to American and World History	Gr. 4-8	12 Titles
The Bright Blue Thinking Books	Gr. 1-6	3 Titles
Building Language Power	Gr. 4-9	3 Titles
EnviroLearn™	Gr. K-5	5 Titles
Foundations for Writing	Gr. 2-8	2 Titles
Home Study Collection™	Gr. 1-6	18 Titles
Inkblots	Gr. K-6	3 Titles
The Little Red Writing Books	Gr. 1-6	3 Titles
Math Whiz Kids™	Gr. 3-5	4 Titles
Novel Extenders	Gr. 1-6	7 Titles
Once Upon A Time™ for Emerging Readers	Gr. K-2	10 Titles
Once Upon A Time™ (Books + Tapes)	Gr. K-2	10 Titles
The Picture Book Companion	Gr. K-3	3 Titles
Quick Thinking™	Gr. K-6	1 Title
Springboards for Reading	Gr. 3-6	2 Titles
Structures for Reading, Writing, Thinking	Gr. 4-9	4 Titles
Test Preparation Guides	Gr. 2-12	41 Titles
Thematic Units	Gr. K-8	23 Titles
Writing Warm-Ups™	Gr. K-6	2 Titles

To order, contact your local school supply store, or write:

ECS Learning Systems, Inc.
P.O. Box 791437
San Antonio, Texas 78279-1437

Editor: Shirley J. Durst
Cover/Page Layout: Kirstin Simpson
Book Design: Educational Media Services

ISBN 1-57022-195-2

Printed in the United States of America.

Authors' Note

Leif Fearn's work with children and writing had its genesis many years ago when his sixth-grade students' fiction ended up as a full page of stories in the local newspaper. Later, in both the Southwest and Northwest, he had the opportunity to emphasize literacy development as a trainer of Head Start teachers and aides. His early applications of creative thinking to existing curriculum, however, eventually led to his and Nancy's conception of Balanced Writing instruction.

Nancy Farnan's teaching began with middle and secondary students in the Midwest. Early in her career, she experienced her students' learning to write as watching buds opening to full bloom—the changes were observable, tangible, and powerful. She was impressed by the power her students discovered as they became increasingly effective writers.

A little over a decade ago, Leif and Nancy began to use their experiences, along with those of several outstanding teachers and colleagues, to develop the concept of Balanced Writing instruction. For a decade they have worked with teachers in the Writing Institute for Teachers at San Diego State University, refining and adding to their conception of what a Balanced Writing program would look and sound like. They have authored and co-authored many books and articles on writing and regularly lead workshops to promote Balanced Writing instruction and literacy.

Today, Leif and Nancy teach at San Diego State University, where they share an office in the School of Teacher Education. As key figures in the development of Balanced Writing instruction, they have devoted their professional lives to literacy and the development of writing skills. Married, Leif and Nancy live in San Diego, California, where they meet regularly with the professional writers' community.

Contents

About This Book

 ## The Get Writing!! Series

The **Get Writing!!** series is a comprehensive, teacher-friendly, Balanced Writing program for kindergarten through fifth grade.

Balanced Writing instruction was born in the late 1970s as Developmental Writing, an application of creative thinking skills to teaching and learning basic school skills and content (Fearn, 1976). Balanced Writing instruction focuses specific attention on balancing three components of writing associated with learning to write well:

1. The **CONTENT** of writing
   • Sentence thinking and writing
   • Thinking and writing in relationships between and among sentences
   • Thinking and writing in paragraphs
   • Progressive mastery of writing for various purposes across the genres
   • Progressive mastery of writing conventions
   • Assessment and editing

2. The **PROCESSES** involved in learning and writing
   • Written interactions between planning and drafting and between drafting and revision
   • Control of the cognitive devices of attention
   • Conceptualization
   • Application of specific creative thinking skills

3. The **TIME** demands
   Practice in Balanced Writing instruction should be 10 percent of the instructional week, or up to 100 to 150 clock minutes of instructional time per week.

 ## What's Inside This Book?

The lessons in **Get Writing!!** relate directly to every student in the room. They specify student writing behaviors, include multiple procedures for the assessment of writing, and describe, in the most explicit terms, what teachers and students can do to achieve each objective.

Get Writing!! Book 2 Grades 2-3, Paragraphs and Forms of Writing, is a Balanced Writing approach to teaching second- and third-grade students to organize their main ideas into paragraphs. Students move from thinking in and writing strings of related sentences from sentence cues, to writing mature paragraphs in autobiographical writing, news writing, story writing, and letter writing. They also learn to revise their paragraphs for clarity and meaning, while maintaining proper capitalization, punctuation, and spelling. Use *Get Writing!! Book 2 Grades 2-3, Paragraphs and Forms of Writing,* with *Get Writing!! Book 1 Grades 2-3, Sentences and Mechanical Control.*

 ## Lesson Design

Each lesson in this book begins with Information for the Teacher and with a section of detailed instructions and examples for conducting the lesson. These examples include a synopsis of student/teacher dialogue based on actual sessions with children and adolescents. For identification purposes, the teacher's comments and questions are enclosed in quotations, and the students' comments are enclosed in parentheses.

Each lesson also includes the following:

- Daily Writing Activities
- Applications of the Lesson Across the Curriculum
- Applications for English Language Learners
- Reproducible Language Activity Sheets for classroom use

As with all other skills, writing skills can be acquired at more than one level of sophistication. Thinking in sentences, for instance, is introduced in *Get Writing!! Kindergarten*, and *Get Writing!! Grade 1*, then applied to writing in *Get Writing!! Books 1 and 2 Grades 2-3*, and again in the *Get Writing!! Books 1 and 2 Grades 4-5* books. Certain activities are appropriate at any grade level. If students claim they "did this last year," they can be reminded that what they remember about writing from last year will give them a running start this year.

 ## Hints for Supporting a Balanced Writing Program

- **Writing instruction should focus young writers' attention on creation (the thinking in writing) and on making the scribal part of writing as automatic as possible.** In writing, practice makes automatic, so some instructional processes should emphasize speed and quantity.

- **Practice makes permanent.** Every instance of writing, no matter the context, the reason, the audience, the genre, the authenticity—every one—is an instance of practice. If we want good writing from our first-, fifth-, and tenth-graders, we have to ensure that they write well every time. Our piano teachers and football coaches have the right idea, but mere practice doesn't make perfect; perfect practice makes perfect.

- **In writing instruction, as in all instruction, certain basic principles of teaching and learning must not be compromised.** First, learners must understand what is being taught. They must understand what they are supposed to do, and how they are supposed to do it. Secondly, good instruction takes advantage of, and honors, the prior knowledge that learners bring to school. Third, because children have three options in the classroom (to approach, to avoid, or to ignore), good teachers make sure most of the children achieve nearly all of the time. This virtually precludes avoiding and ignoring.

Get Writing!!
Paragraphs and
Forms of Writing

- **Call activities by their right names and frame directions in the vocabulary of writing.**

  Example: "That's a sentence, Eric. Read it again. Everyone, listen to Eric's sentence."

- **Avoid complex definitions.** For example, if you want a complex sentence, it isn't necessary to define dependent and independent clauses and the relationship(s) between the two. Instead, prompt students to think of a sentence in which the first word is *although*. Then, direct them to listen to examples from other students in the room. Call attention to accurate models and reinforce.

- **Never give more time to write than young writers need.** If they are given five minutes, four will need six; if they are given six, three of the four will need seven. If they are given one minute, they'll think they can't do it, but most will. Everyone, novice and expert alike, can produce written language a whole lot faster and better than they think they can. An important part of learning to write is experiencing our own ability to achieve.

- **All writers must take full responsibility for spelling accurately, but don't let students' inability to spell a word correctly interfere with writing their draft.** At this point, the message to students must be, "Spell as well as you can."

- **Everything in this book is about fluency, precision, quantity, and quality at the same time.** Getting it down on paper and getting it right are not opposites, and neither one compromises the other. Monitor students' writing by standing behind them as they read aloud.

  Example: "Put a comma right here, Cheryl. Boys and girls, remember that we always use commas when we write sentences that contain items in a series."

- **Avoid putting young writers in the position of having to live up to perfection.** Rather than saying, "That's the best paragraph in the world, Ramon," say, "That's a terrific paragraph, Ramon. Read it again."

- **Make sure that what most of the writing students do is both oral and written (scribal).** Part of learning to write is establishing the sound of good writing.

  Example: "Read it again, Margo, and everyone listen to the sound of Margo's sentence."

©ECS Learning Systems, Inc., San Antonio, TX

 ## Portfolios

A portfolio is a collection of work, often one's "Best Efforts." There is little or no reason for having writing portfolios in classrooms where children and young adolescents don't write much, but in classrooms where they do, they need a place to keep and organize their work.

Young writers write an enormous amount in this program. They write every day across content areas and through the genres, both collaboratively and alone. Youngsters who write this much need a place to collect, organize, and reflect upon their work. It is recommended that each student in this program keep and maintain a writing portfolio (Farnan and Fearn, 1994).

 ## English Language Learners

Every lesson in the **Get Writing!!** series has a section describing applications for children who do not speak English as a native language. Our experience and research shows that the Balanced Writing instruction represented in this program is successful with non-native speakers of English. The oral language component of the program embedded in every lesson is especially important for students whose native language is not English.

 ## Children and Young Adolescents with Special Needs

The first formal study of the impact of balanced writing instruction was conducted with learning disabled elementary school children (Prior, 1979). Focusing on developmental student performance tends to cut through the various "disabling" conditions. Given prior assessment of suitability to the skill level of the students, the activities in the **Get Writing!!** series are entirely appropriate for special needs youngsters.

 ## Home Schoolers

Balanced writing instruction has been used successfully by home school parents for many years. It is linguistically rigorous and intellectually demanding. It can be handled on a whole class, small group, or individual basis. The procedures associated with each lesson in this book are clear and focus on the developmental performance of young writers. While no collection of instructional materials is appropriate for everyone under all circumstances, this program contains literacy activities that have been used under a vast array of circumstances, including the home school setting.

Get Writing!! Book 2 Grades 2-3   ©ECS Learning Systems, Inc., San Antonio, TX   ix

1 How Sentences Become Paragraphs

—A paragraph is a string of written language that features a main idea.

 ## Information for the Teacher

- A paragraph must have a main idea.

- A paragraph need not have a topic sentence.

- A paragraph need not have a specified number of sentences of any specified kind(s).

- A paragraph is defined by its main idea. That is all.

This lesson emphasizes the development of a main idea in **strings of sentences**. The main idea in one sentence becomes a main idea displayed in two sentences, then a main idea displayed in three sentences. Eventually, the main idea is developed enough to be a paragraph.

It is very important that young writers understand early on that the main idea is the **controlling characteristic** in writing paragraphs. In later grades, they will begin to understand the paragraph as an organizational device rather than a composing device; a way to conceptualize ideas and images, rather than something to write deliberately.

 ## Objective

Young writers will think in and produce related sentences and focus, in discussion, on the developing main idea. The result of the activity will be writings that clearly focus on a primary, or main, idea.

    ©ECS Learning Systems, Inc., San Antonio, TX

 ## Conducting the Lesson

1. **Give students a sentence cue. Ask them to construct a sentence in their heads.**

    Example: "Think of a sentence in which there is a truck. It can be any sort of truck, and that's the only idea that you must have in your sentence. Write your sentence in your head first, and then on paper. In a few seconds I will give you a chance to read what you have written."

2. **Ask the children to read their sentences, focusing on the main idea in each one.** Listen to several sentences, and each time ask the reader to identify the image or idea. Each time a young writer is able to tell the image or idea, reinforce with the term *main idea*.

    Example: "Yes, the main idea in Eric's sentence is the red truck he got for his birthday. The image, the picture, of the truck is the main idea in the sentence. Every sentence has a main idea."

3. **Listen to several sentences, and each time solicit the image or idea.** Each time a young writer is able to tell the image or idea, reinforce with the term *main idea*.

4. **On the following day, or when the children are ready to handle the next step, introduce a second sentence to go with the first one.**

    Example: "Remember the truck sentence and how we were making sentences that contained a main idea? Well, now we're going to make the sentence just a little bigger. This time I want you to think of a sentence that has a truck in it, but I also want a mountain in it. So now we have a sentence that contains a truck *and* a mountain." [Solicit readings, comment, and reinforce as in Numbers 1 and 2, above.]

5. **Over time, lead young writers to automatically think in and write in their heads, as well as on paper, sentences with two or three given ideas (*truck, mountain, tree, road, orange,* and so forth).** In preparation for the next step in the process, it is also useful for young writers to think in and write sentences with the given ideas (truck and so forth) in reverse order.

 Cue

Write one (then two, then three) sentences which include the following ideas....

6. **When it is clear that most of the children are writing single sentences automatically and well, direct them to think about how to write two sentences in a row using the ideas on the board.**

   Example: "Think of a way to put these two ideas (*truck* and *mountain*) into two related sentences in a row."

7. **Ask students to listen as a volunteer reads his/her sentence string aloud.** Then ask children to tell what the main idea or image is.

   Example: The red truck had apples in the back. The driver was taking the apples down the mountain to the store.

8. **Ask a volunteer to read only the second sentence and to notice how the two sentences relate to the main idea.** The key to this stage of paragraphing is the concept of main idea. Direct the classroom conversation to the main idea.

   Example: "Now read just your second sentence." (**The driver was taking the apples down the mountain to the store**.) "How was the driver getting down the mountain?" (In the truck.) "How do we know that?" (It's in the first sentence.) "Yes, that's right. The two sentences work together to make the main idea, the main image. You did that very well. You made the sentences work together."

9. **When students are able to make "doubles" that work together to make main ideas or images the audience is able to articulate, add a third sentence to the process.** Conduct the session(s) as in steps 1-5. Write three ideas on the board or overhead (*snow, ski, cloud, forest*, etc.). Ask the students to think of a way to arrange the ideas in three related sentences. Follow the procedures above for reading, commenting, and discussing main ideas.

10. **Debrief.** The final stage of the activity is thinking about the possibility of a final sentence in the "string." Having written three sentences, and having discussed how the main idea from the first sentence expanded in size and detail, ask, "Is the main idea finished, or do you think there should be another sentence?"

For early second-graders, getting ready for the multiple sentences stage of the process takes as long as a month or so. For mid- to late third-graders, it can be only a day or two.

©ECS Learning Systems, Inc., San Antonio, TX

 Daily Writing Activities

Daily activities are posed in the form of one, two, and three idea sets that can be used to promote single, double, and triple sentence sessions. Sift and select to suit what you think will make sense to the children in your class. Remember, there need not be a particular relationship between and among the ideas, for young and not-so-young writers will make the connections in clever ways.

1. small, musical, send
2. square, village, table
3. rest, picture, block
4. sheet, fresh, open
5. wish, yell, neighborhood
6. sleep, pilot, coast
7. relative, jump, steam
8. skill, rock, blind
9. wolf, moon, alone
10. talk, river, streak

11. gone, flower, water
12. right, pain, salt
13. dance, sweet, attic
14. chip, stamp, stack
15. blush, quiet, fly
16. push, town, airport
17. band, slip, change
18. rain, fish, green
19. growth, peace, lake
20. lose, house, story

 Tip

This paragraphing activity may consume several months, as children are drawn into a sense of how a main idea can get larger and more detailed as sentences are added.

Early second-graders may take the better part of several months to achieve a three-sentence string in the deliberate manner described above. Later, in the second or third grade, learning to write in a three-sentence string may be accomplished within several weeks.

Get Writing!! Book 2 Grades 2-3   ©ECS Learning Systems, Inc., San Antonio, TX   13

 Across the Curriculum

To apply this activity to another subject area, select words in any unit the class is studying at the moment. For example, if they are studying an ecology unit, the children might write a description of material they see through a low-power microscope.

As the children call out their observations, write them on the board. Direct each student to select three of the ideas from the list on the board and apply what they have learned during the writing period. Ask them to compose a three-sentence string about what they observed.

When they have written several three-sentence strings and those have been shared, ask "paragraph" questions:

- Do you need another sentence to finish your paragraph?

- What is the main idea of your paragraph?

- Is there one sentence that best tells about the main idea?

©ECS Learning Systems, Inc., San Antonio, TX

English Language Learners

Children learning English need an opportunity to engage in the sounds of the language. In this lesson, an explicit oral component exists in the drafting and planning or in the drafting and revising interactions.

On one occasion, 27 second-graders were allowed to do the activities in whichever language felt most comfortable. Several of the non-English speakers chose to write in their native language. When a bilingual child shared in a language other than English, one of the others translated for the teacher and translated directions back to the child. The teacher then directed the young writer to rethink the oral sentence(s) and deliver them in English as well as his or her native language. When it came time to write the sentence on paper, permission to write in the native language was given again, but the reading still occurred in both languages.

Language Activity Sheet

How Sentences Become Paragraphs

1. Think of a sentence that contains the idea of *farmer*. First write the sentence in your head. Then copy the sentence you have written in your head in the blanks.

____

____

____

2. Think of a way to add something about animals to the sentence about the farmer. Remember, first you think, then you write your idea.

____

____

____

3. Write the main idea of the sentence you wrote for Number 2. Don't rewrite the sentence. Write just the main idea.

____

____

____

4. Write two sentences in a row that include the ideas of *farmer* and *animals*.

_____

_____

_____

5. Write the main idea of your double-sentence string.

_____

_____

6. Write three sentences in a row about the ideas of farmer and animals, and an idea about something else you might find on a farm.

_____

_____

_____

_____

_____

7. Write the main idea for the three sentences you wrote for Number 6.

_____

_____

8. Is your paragraph finished? If it isn't, write a sentence on the other side of this page that you think will finish it.

2 Related Sentences

—If there is a main idea, there is a paragraph; if there isn't a main idea, there isn't a paragraph.

 ## Information for the Teacher

All of the "building blocks" in teaching paragraphs are important only if a main idea exists. The building blocks alone won't make a paragraph. Everything from *topic sentence* to *detail sentences* and *terminals* or *transitionals* is secondary to main idea.

The step-by-step procedure in **Related Sentences** virtually guarantees that early second-graders will be able to write a paragraph on the very first attempt. The paragraph is written in a small group, or as a whole class under the teacher's direction.

 ## Objective

Young writers will compose a paragraph on the very first attempt, and the critical terminology, *main idea*, will be an explicit part of the writing, the thinking, and the teacher's questions and commentary.

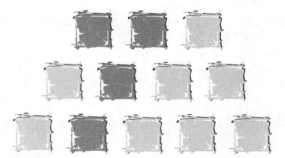

 It is very important that students in the early stages of writing understand paragraphs as larger pieces of meaning, rather than as combinations of specified kinds of sentences in a specified order, configuration, or image on the page (e.g., the five-sentence formula, detail sentences followed by explanatory sentences).

 Conducting the Lesson

1. **Draw a row of three boxes on the board. Write the word** *boy* **in the second box.** Ask for a volunteer to think of a three-word sentence with "boy" as the second word.

   Example: The boy cried.

2. **Make a four-box row just below the first sentence.** Ask the students to create a second sentence with four words. In the four boxes on the board, write a volunteer's oral sentence.

   Example: "The first sentence is about a boy crying. What might be the next sentence in four words?" (**He cried very loud.**) [In this case, put the ending on the adverb *loudly*. Don't make an issue of it. Just write the word correctly and read the sentence aloud: "**He cried very loudly.**"]

3. **Ask the students to identify the main idea of the four-word sentence.** Ask, "What is this story about? What's happening here?" These questions are about main idea. Solicit several possibilities. Explain to the class that there is no single, unambiguous right answer or main idea. There are many possibilities. (In the example sentence above, the boy could have fallen. He could have been stung by a bee. He could be lost. He could be angry. He could be frightened. He could be happy to see his father.)

4. **Make a five-box row below the four-word sentence.** Ask a volunteer to suggest a five-word sentence. Typically someone gives a sentence about why the boy is crying. (**He fell off his bicycle.**) However, after listening to several sentences, you may need to suggest that the main idea of the five-word sentence is about *why* the boy is crying. This isn't completely "natural" writing, but it may promote the quality of a paragraph being constructed on this first try.

Think of a three-word sentence in which the second word is
_____ . Write a four-word sentence to follow the three-word sentence. Then write a five-word sentence. Finish the paragraph with a final sentence.

Related Sentences

5. **Ask the students to complete the paragraph by writing a final sentence that contains as many words as they choose.**

    Example: "Now, boys and girls, let's finish our paragraph. We need one last sentence for today's paragraph. What do you think it should be? Wanda?" (How many words do we get?) "This time you get as many words as you like." (**The boy ran home and went to the doctor**.)

6. **Ask for volunteers to read the sentences aloud and to identify the main idea of the paragraph.**

    Example: "Let's read our paragraph, boys and girls. Someone read it for us." (**The boy cried. He cried very loudly. He fell off his bicycle. The boy ran home and went to the doctor.**) "What do you think the paragraph is about? What is the main idea?"

7. **Slip the term** *main idea* **in with "what the paragraph is about."** The terms are interchangeable, and the children can "hook into" whichever term makes sense.

8. **Debrief.** Remind students that they will write many more paragraphs in the next several weeks, and we will think about main ideas and the details that help us understand what they are about.

There is no implication here that paragraphs must have four sentences. If several days or weeks of the four-sentence design suggests to you that the children will over-generalize to four-sentence paragraphs, vary it immediately, or as soon as you think it is appropriate.

 Daily Writing Activities

The **Related Sentences** strategy, as entrée into paragraphs in the late primary grades, operates on the basis of a three-word sentence as an opener, followed by a sentence of four-words, then five-words, and then a sentence of indeterminate length. Any of the following three openers will work as described in the procedures on pages 19 and 20.

1. Write a three-word sentence in which the second word is *rain*.

2. Write a three-word sentence in which the second word is *girl*.

3. Write a three-word sentence in which the second word is *plant*.

After years of experience with second- and third-graders writing sentences of specified length with specific words in stated positions, it is clear that seven- and eight-year-olds can make position switches very well once they develop some experience with the manipulation. Try openers such as the following:

4. Write a three-word sentence in which the first word is *boys*.

5. Write a three-word sentence in which the third word is *rain*.

6. Write a three-word sentence in which the third word is *plants*.

7. Write a three-word sentence in which the first word is *plant*. (The children will have to pay attention here. The sentence will be somewhat different from the traditional declarative so common in early writing procedures.)

8. Write a four-word sentence in which *water* is in the fourth position.

9. Write a four-word sentence in which *water* is in the second position. (Place the given word, *water*, in the first, then third positions, as well.)

10. Write a five-word sentence in which *car* is in the second position.

Tip

This is not to say that young writers should not eventually move from a three- to a four- or a five-word opener. Give them several sessions to get accustomed to the four-word design. Then, with attention still focused on main idea and paragraph development, try opening with a four-word sentence, moving to a five-word, then a six-word, and finally a closing sentence of indeterminate length.

Get Writing!! Book 2 Grades 2-3 ©ECS Learning Systems, Inc., San Antonio, TX   21

Related Sentences

 Across the Curriculum

Related Sentences is an excellent strategy for moving young writers into "theme-based" writing where the purpose is a tight, single, main-idea piece. In science, an activity in an extended unit on plant life and its effect on the air we breathe might be introduced in this way: "Write a four-word sentence in which the word *oxygen* appears in the fifth position. Now, thinking about what we have been studying and talking about, what do you think might be a six-word sentence that comes next?"

Continue the activity on the board through three, four, five, maybe even six sentences, focusing throughout on identifying and exploring a single main idea. When the youngsters have finished the paragraph on the board, they should all write it on their own paper with the freedom to make any changes they want along the way. On another day, set up the activity on the board with another main idea (plant growth and sunlight, for instance), but encourage them to write their own sentences as you lead the activity at the board.

 English Language Learners

Learning is an act of construction, and children, whether they are English speakers in French language schools or Spanish or Navajo speakers in English language schools, face the task of constructing both content and language. The best of all possible worlds would be a learning situation in which both kinds of constructions occur not just simultaneously but in service to each other; that is, where the construction of language serves the content.

Related Sentences is such an activity. There is a structure in the language portion of the activity that promotes construction within comfortable boundaries. In addition, there is an opportunity to think in the content under study, so the fact that the children's comfort zone is not in English does not, by definition, compromise content learning.

Language Activity Sheet
Related Sentences

1. Think of a three-word sentence with *girl* as the second word. Fill in the blanks on the first line with your words. Then write a four-word and five-word sentence to make a paragraph.

_____ girl _____

_____ _____ _____ _____

_____ _____ _____ _____ _____

2. What might be the final sentence in the paragraph?

_____

_____

_____

3. Rewrite your paragraph on the lines below. Notice that the first line in the paragraph is indented.

_____

_____

_____

_____

4. Fill in the blanks to make the first two sentences of a paragraph.

_____ *sand* _____ _____ _____

_____ _____ _____ _____ _____ _____

5. What might be the final sentence in the paragraph?

_____

_____

_____

6. What is the main idea of the paragraph?

_____

_____

_____

3 Paragraph Completion

—As they write, writers manage, manipulate, organize, and reorganize sentences to support their new ideas.

 ## Information for the Teacher

Paragraph Completion bridges the gap between sentence writing, which the children can already do, and paragraph writing, or writing multiple sentences in a pattern. The multiple sentence task is complex on the first try, and the additional task of sentence patterning may overload some children.

Writing good paragraphs is not too difficult a task for second- and third-graders, but it is a lot to handle at once. However, if instruction is delayed, by the time children get to the age or maturity to put it all together, many come to believe paragraphs are some sort of mysterious writing only teachers know about.

In **Paragraph Completion**, young writers will successfully think and write in main idea context and paragraphs. They can do it because the stage is set with the first sentence and sentence stem prompts that eliminate the need to invent whole sentences while trying to explore a single idea.

 ## Objective

Young writers will think in and write a paragraph on the basis of a three-sentence format. They will begin with an initial sentence and two stems, in time progress to three stems, and finally, use a cue such as, "Write a paragraph in which the main idea is …."

©ECS Learning Systems, Inc., San Antonio, TX

 ## Conducting the Lesson

1. **On the board or an overhead screen, show a paragraph completion design:**

    Example: Ben searched and searched. Suddenly he saw … Down the street …

2. **Ask students to read along as a volunteer reads the sentence and sentence stems aloud.** After they speculate what the cue may be about, or what the main idea might be, ask them to write a paragraph so one of the main ideas will come through, beginning with the second sentence.

    Example: "Okay, let's write to your main idea. You said you thought the main idea was that Ben lost his dog. The first sentence in the paragraph reads, **Ben searched and searched**. Since it is your main idea, how do you think the second sentence should be finished? Remember, it begins, **Suddenly he saw ….** How do you think it will end?" (**… his dog.**) "Let's make the whole sentence. It begins, **Suddenly he saw …** what about his dog?" (**Suddenly he saw his dog running away.**)

> **Tip**
>
> Notice no definition of *main idea* or *paragraph* is given to the students at this point. Those terms simply become part of the conversation. As the children become increasingly adroit with paragraph writing, there will be some conversation about terms and definitions.

3. **Write the student's second sentence on the board and ask a volunteer to read it. Then ask another volunteer to speculate what the last sentence of the paragraph might be.**

    Example: "Someone read the paragraph so far." (**Ben searched and searched. Suddenly he saw his dog running away.**) "The next sentence begins, **Down the street ….** What do you think the rest of the sentence should be?" (**Down the street he could see his dog running as fast as he could go.**)

4. **After the student reads the sentence, ask, how the paragraph might end.**

    Example: "What do you think the last sentence in the paragraph might be?" (**Ben was very sad because his dog ran away.**)

> **Cue**
>
> Pose a paragraph design on an overhead or the board with an opening sentence followed by two sentence stems. Young writers speculate on the main idea and complete the sentence stems to conform to their speculations.

Get Writing!! Book 2 Grades 2-3 ©ECS Learning Systems, Inc., San Antonio, TX 27

Paragraph Completion

5. **Read the whole paragraph to the class now, and direct the student to read along.** Acknowledge the student for writing a paragraph and remind the class that paragraphs always have main ideas.

   Example: "What is the main idea of your paragraph?" (His dog ran away.) "Do you think the dog will be lost?" (Yeah, but Ben will find him later.) "So the main idea is that the dog ran away, not that the dog is lost?" (Uh-huh.) "You wrote a paragraph. Good for you. A paragraph always has a main idea."

6. **At the next writing time, pose another Paragraph Completion model on the board or overhead screen.**

   Example: The sun shone brightly. The children were having a good time at …. They all were ready to play ….

7. **Again, ask students to speculate about what the main idea might be.** After listening to several ideas, ask them to write the first sentence. Respond to the inevitable questions about spelling by reminding them that the whole sentence is on the board and all the words are spelled correctly there.

   Example: "What do you think this paragraph might be about? What do you think the main idea might be?" [Listen to several responses and comment as you feel appropriate.] "Yesterday we wrote a paragraph together on the board. Today I would like you to write your own paragraph. Let's begin with the first sentence. Write the first sentence on your paper about the sun shining brightly."

8. **Ask the students to put their pencils down and think of what a good second sentence might be.** Pause, then give them one minute to write this sentence on their paper. The one-minute time period is designed to send the message to write deliberately.

Tip

Notice the emphasis here, as the young writers speculate on main ideas before writing and after the fact. It is not necessary for these main ideas to be the same, as writer's ideas often change during writing. On this first paragraph attempt, it is sufficient to "notice" changes, rather than call attention to them or ask the students to manage their sentences so the main idea will remain the same.

Paragraph Completion

9. **Repeat the preceding steps for the third sentence, allowing for the possibility that there might be more to write.**

   Example: "If you think you need another sentence to finish your paragraph, write it in your head first so you can hear what it sounds like with the other sentences."

Tip

Watch carefully, and when it appears most of the children are finished or nearly finished, tell the students to prepare to read their sentences. After another 30 seconds, even if some are not finished, have students read their sentences. Comment as appropriate.

10. **Solicit readers, and in the comments following each reading, solicit speculations from the writer about main idea.** Ask others about the main idea being read aloud. Have a conversation about main ideas.

11. **Conduct a new paragraph completion activity twice a week for several weeks.** In a relatively short time, the children will be able to write to the cue in several minutes and engage in reasonably insightful conversation after the readings.

12. **After a paragraph has been written, read it aloud, discuss briefly, and broaden the discussion by asking a variety of questions,** "What do you think might be the first sentence of the next paragraph? What do you think might be the main idea of the next paragraph? What do you think might be the main idea of the paragraph just before the one you just wrote?" Focus on main idea throughout the discussion.

Tip

The basic procedure here ensures, first, that most of the children write a paragraph every time—one that reads like a paragraph and contains a discernable main idea. Although the activity introduces young writers to the matter of transition from paragraph to paragraph, do not make an issue of prior and following main ideas. Such discussion is merely introductory; they do not have to know the answer to Number 12, above.

Get Writing!! Book 2 Grades 2-3

Paragraph Completion

 ## Daily Writing Activities

The following are several paragraph completion "designs" which can be used and adjusted over several weeks. Each of these paragraph completion designs can be handled just as in the procedures described in the previous lesson.

1. **Marcy and Jim skipped down the street to the playground. Along the way they saw …. It ran toward them ….**

2. **In the morning the sun shone brightly. The girls ate their breakfast and …. When the bus honked its horn ….**

3. **Blue was her favorite color. She told the children …. They were all very happy to hear ….**

Below are several designs in which the first sentence is also a sentence stem which young writers need to complete. Now they are faced with an even greater task in speculating on main ideas.

1. **One day long ago …. The giant birds …. When the eggs hatched ….**

2. **All the children rode together over …. They had been thinking about this trip …. They knew it would be the best ….**

3. **Everyone knew there was a truck outside because …. They wanted to see …. But it was reading time, and the teacher ….**

30   Get Writing!! Book 2 Grades 2-3   ©ECS Learning Systems, Inc., San Antonio, TX

In this activity, direct the children to add the "next" sentence in order to "finish" the paragraph. It is important that while the first two of the following activities lead the children to four-sentence paragraphs, they "learn" that all paragraphs do not have four sentences. Notice that the third activity leads children to a five-sentence paragraph.

1. **Elbert was having a good time at the party when all of a sudden he .... Nothing he could say would make his mother .... She took him into the house and ....** (What do you think might be the next sentence that will finish the paragraph?)

2. **Rachel didn't want to wear the sweater, but her mother .... It made Rachel very angry because .... Today was her birthday, and ....** (What do you think might be the next sentence that will finish the paragraph?)

3. **The monster was huge and yellow, but .... He stood above the .... It roared and everyone ....** (What do you think might be the next two sentences that will finish the paragraph?)

For paragraph completion purposes, the activity continues into higher and higher levels of complexity by shrinking the amount of information provided in the sentence stems so young writers have to deliver greater and greater proportions of the paragraphs. However, the material above is sufficient for most young second- and third-grade writers.

Paragraph Completion

 Across the Curriculum

If learning is construction and writing is a constructive process, it is likely that young students construct knowledge by writing about it. The social studies program, for example, includes information about the beginnings of the nation—the landing of Europeans, the first winter, relationships with indigenous people, exploring the wilderness, and so forth. Within this lesson, there might be paragraph completion tasks such as the following:

When the first settlers came to the shores of the New World, they found …. People lived on the land and …. During the first winter ….

©ECS Learning Systems, Inc., San Antonio, TX

English Language Learners

One of the keys to teaching children whose native language is not English is providing comprehensible input. This means the children must understand what teachers ask them to do and how to do it.

Everyone can understand main idea. In paragraph completion, young writers are provided with the opening sentence and one or more sentence stems to complete. They can focus their attention on main idea, not on various kinds of sentences and architectural patterns. This allows them to become comfortable writing paragraphs without having to struggle with attributes that can even be problematic for children whose native language is English.

Approximation, a second attribute of paragraph completion, satisfies the comprehensible input requirement for second language acquisition and management. Young writers move in stages or approximations toward paragraph writing.

Tip

To write their first whole paragraph, students begin with a main idea, and with sentence cues provided, write to that main idea. Over time, as less and less material is provided, they will write more and more on their own terms.

          33

Language Activity Sheet
Paragraph Completion

1. Read the sentence in the box and think about what the main idea of the sentence might be.

> **The boy was very tired when he got home from the game.**

2. Write what you think the main idea of a paragraph will be if the sentence in the box above is the first sentence.

_____

3. Finish the sentence in the box below so it can be part of a paragraph about the boy who was tired after going to the game.

> **He sat down for ...**

_____

_____

4. Finish the next sentence in the box so it can be the fourth sentence about the tired boy.

> **After dinner ...**

_____

_____

 ©ECS Learning Systems, Inc., San Antonio, TX

5. Write the last sentence for the paragraph about the tired boy.

_____

_____

6. Read your paragraph and write what you think the main idea is.

_____

_____

7. Now write the paragraph on the lines below. You may change words or even whole sentences.

_____

_____

_____

_____

_____

4 Autobiographical Writing

—People learn to write so they can make and save messages and send messages to others.

 ## Information for the Teacher

Children do not learn to write so they can write sentences and paragraphs. They learn to write so they can make and send messages. They make messages to send to other people, sometimes to their teachers, their friends, and even to themselves. Sometimes people also make messages only for the purpose of recording and saving information or thoughts and feelings.

This writing activity seems quite similar to diaries and journals, with entries selected by the writer. However, at least in the beginning stages, the teacher determines the direction for this activity. Young writers can write in two genres at once (daily journal and/or diary entries, as well as responses to autobiographical cues), using their journals to write even more extensively, perhaps reflecting their feelings about the teacher's cue or prompt.

 ## Objective

Young writers will write several times each week in response to cues about their own experiences. The purpose of **Autobiographical Writing** is to habituate reflective writing and help young writers acquire the pattern of recording their life experiences.

©ECS Learning Systems, Inc., San Antonio, TX

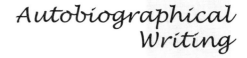

 Conducting the Lesson

1. **Choose two days a week for autobiographical writing.** Announce to the class that they will be doing this kind of writing two days a week throughout the year.

2. **Place a red box of 8 1/2" X 5 1/2" paper (lined for primary grade-level) on a table in the room.** Explain to the students that if they write carefully, they will be able to write all they have to on one side of the paper.

3. **Refer to the cue or prompt on the board, directing students to think of things that make them laugh.** Then ask them to choose one thing that makes them laugh and to write about it on one side of the paper.

   Example: "Choose one of the things that makes you laugh. Think about it. Remember when it happened. Think about how it happened. Think about who was there. Think about how you felt. Think about everything you could say about that time when something happened that made you laugh."

   Hand out the 8 1/2" X 5 1/2" sheets of paper from the red box. Give the students five minutes to write as much as they can and as well as they can. (Remind them to ask three classmates before asking the teacher when they have a question during writing time. Also, remind them to figure out the spelling so they will be able to read it later and correct it.)

   There may be questions, and it will be frustrating when some of the children feel they need to ask about everything. However, as the year goes on, the children will acquire more and more independence as fluency is expected and required.

Think of something that makes you laugh. Write about something that makes you laugh.

Autobiographical Writing

4. **At the end of the five minutes, ask the children to find a good place to stop.** Explain that during their independent time they must finish the piece as their Ticket to Recess. Ask them to drop their "ticket" in the red box as they leave the room for recess. Such a plan begins a measure of independence in writing assignments.

> The Ticket to Recess idea is a moderately difficult one to get off the ground, but once established, it causes children to take responsibility for their own work and behavior. The first recess or two, a few children may not have a ticket, but all they have to do is sit down and write. This isn't punishment, it is merely the ticket out of the room.

5. **Allow a couple of days to pass, then prepare another cue or prompt on the board.** Put paper in the red box. As the children file into the room that morning, show everyone the red box on the table, the prompt on the board, and tell them the paper will be the Ticket to Recess. When morning exercises are finished, make the announcement again. Conduct a short preparatory conversation about the cue or prompt.

   Example: "Think of something that happened to you recently that made you feel good."

6. **During the morning, give perhaps two reminders about the paper and the ticket to recess.**

> Spot-read these autobiographical papers and turn them back to the children for inclusion in their writing portfolios. Select several to post on the board for several days, then take them down and return them to their owners. Occasionally, post all the papers, calling attention to where they are and the necessity of reading them. Because these papers are about the **most important topic** in the class (the children), there is an increased probability they will be read.
>
> We also recommend that teachers give young writers the opportunity to read their writings to small groups or in a whole-class setting. Let the writer sit in front of the group (or class) from an "Author's Chair." When the writer is finished, the other children can ask questions, comment on what they liked, and tell what they would like to know more about. The writer can then revise if he/she chooses.

 ©ECS Learning Systems, Inc., San Antonio, TX

 ## Daily Writing Activities

1. I'm young, and there are some things I don't understand. This is about something I don't understand.

2. Do you know how to be "quick" about doing something? Well, I do.

3. I can write something about "Someday I'm going to …."

4. Most of the time I am proud of being a good person. I feel I am a good person when ….

5. This is my favorite holiday.

6. I am often a happy person. I am happiest when ….

7. I can think of a time when I liked the dark.

8. I can speak two languages. Being able to speak two languages helps me ….

9. Sometimes I feel creative. I remember when I felt creative.

10. This is about something I do at home that shows I am a responsible person.

11. I like to spend time with my family doing ….

12. I like myself because ….

13. If I could spend all of my time at school doing one thing, it would be….

14. This is something I learned how to do because I worked very hard on it.

15. I remember when I solved a problem. This is how I did it.

16. My best time of day is ….

17. I know a lot of things. This is something I know well enough to teach someone else. This is how I would teach it.

18. This is about the best book I have ever read.

19. These are some reasons why I am a good person to have as a friend.

20. Sometimes I have arguments with other people. When that happens, I feel ….

Get Writing!! Book 2 Grades 2-3   ©ECS Learning Systems, Inc., San Antonio, TX   39

Across the Curriculum

An autobiographical piece can cover an enormous variety of topics, cues, and areas of emphasis. Notice Activities 1, 8, 9, 11, 13, 14, 15, 17, and 18. Each of these can be related to learning in a content area. Consider Activity 17:

I know a lot of things. This is something I know well enough to teach to someone else. This is how I would teach it.

Consider the following cues or prompts as ways to approach the activity:

1. I can explain directions for solving the number fact: (40 - 26). (Mathematics)

2. Write the story of the Pilgrims' first winter as if you lived there with them. (History)

3. Write about how you learned to predict how many pennies you could put in a clay boat before it would sink. (Mathematics)

4. Write about how you find the way from school to home. (Geography)

Self-reflections, which may involve writing directions, are marvelous opportunities for writing across the curriculum. Students can describe how they learned something or what they learned.

 English Language Learners

When working with children whose native language is not English, it is important to accommodate learners' needs. Those needs can be addressed, at least in part, by making the instruction comprehensible, by focusing on communicating real messages, and by reducing the anxiety associated with working in a second language.

Because autobiographical pieces are about people with whom children are most familiar and situations with which they have direct knowledge, such writing is an anxiety reducer. Furthermore, the entire purpose of such writing is the real and whole message, taking advantage of the cultural foundations and experiences children bring to the classroom from their homes and neighborhoods.

In autobiographical writing, a story may be best told (written) in a student's native language. This is an excellent opportunity to help students understand that their native language works perfectly well in school, in learning, and in expressing learning. It is an open opportunity to express memories and passions in the language that seems more appropriate and/or more comfortable.

Autobiographical Writing

1. Think of something you know how to do. Write its name or what it is in the blank.

   _____

2. Think about how you learned to do what you wrote in the blank above. Think about who taught you or if you learned it all by yourself. Write how you learned it in the spaces below.

   _____

   _____

   _____

3. Think about how it felt when you learned what you wrote in number 1 above. Think back to that time. How did you feel about learning it?

   _____

   _____

   _____

42   *Get Writing!! Book 2 Grades 2-3*   ©ECS Learning Systems, Inc., San Antonio, TX

4. Use the ideas in Numbers 1, 2, and 3 to write about something you know how to do. Write at least three sentences. Be sure to tell what you learned, how you learned it, and how it made you feel to learn it.

_____

_____

_____

_____

5. After you have written about what you know how to do, find a partner and a private place, and read your papers aloud to each other. Switch Language Activity Sheets with your partner and write on your partner's paper what you noticed: **This is what I noticed when I listened to the paper written by my partner**.

_____

_____

6. Ask your partner to write one more thing on your Language Activity Sheet: **This is what my partner's paper made me think about or reminded me of**.

_____

_____

5 Writing About Reading

—*One major purpose of literature is to give readers an opportunity to "wrap their minds and souls around words," to engage in, identify with, and personalize literature for themselves.*

Information for the Teacher

The cues below promote personalizing, identifying, and engaging in and with literature. Notice, as well, that the three cues cover three kinds of responses to literature.

- When children are asked to "think about what they noticed," they tend to think about images and ideas they find important, interesting, or perhaps even confusing. (**I noticed the rabbits jumping over the hound dog and the dog was whining in his sleep**).

- When they're asked **what the piece reminds them of**, they are making personal connections. (**I was at my grandpa's last summer in Iowa, and I remember the barn. We played all day in the piles of hay.**)

- When they are asked **how they feel**, they are responding affectively to the literature. (**At the end the boy had the barn dance singing in his head like the sugarplums at Christmas. That makes me happy because sometimes there are good things singing to me in my head, too.**)

Writing About Reading is a way for young writers to respond to what they read or what is read to them. This is not a traditional book report or an open-ended and often obtuse write-whatever-you-want-to-write prompt. In any writing program it is important to remember that writing goes on in the head before it is pushed out of our mouths or our pencils. In this activity young writers can respond to the cues or prompts both orally and in writing.

Objective

Young writers will respond to what they read and what is read to them in ways that promote both literal and inferential comprehension. They will talk about and write what they notice in the literature, and they will respond to the literature in terms of how it makes them feel and what it reminds them of. These responses to literature, which can be both oral and written, should be a regular part of classroom discussions about literature.

 ## Conducting the Lesson

1. **Read a book to the class.** On the first reading children just listen without looking at the illustrations. Encourage them to create their own images and pictures in their heads and to share orally what they noticed in the story.

    Example: [After reading aloud Audrey Wood's *Elbert's Bad Word* (Harcourt Brace Jovanovich, 1988), ask students to think about the story.] "What do you notice in the book? What do you notice about the story?" (I like the part where the eggs fell on the lady.) "Yes, that's something pretty noticeable. What did you notice?" (How the bad word went away at the end.) (The gardener making the cake with the bad word in it.) "What do you think the bad word looks like, boys and girls?" (It's brown and all prickly. It has long hairs and fleas.) "That certainly looks like something bad to me."

2. **Referring to the cues below, ask the class to write about what they noticed in the reading.**

    Example: "Now, I would like you to write about what you noticed in *Elbert's Bad Word*. I want you to write one or two sentences that tell what you noticed. I have a bulletin board right inside the door, and you can see it has new paper on it. I'm going to put *Elbert's Bad Word* at the top, and we will put the papers with what you noticed right there on the board."

3. **Read *Elbert's Bad Word* again later in the day or the next day and ask the students to think about what the story reminds them of in their own lives.** Separate the class into groups to discuss their responses. Then ask them to write about it and to put their papers in the red box when they are finished.

There are variations on these three questions or cues; but no matter the variation, the key is for youngsters to think about and talk or write about:

- What they notice in a story

- The connections they make with the reading

- The feelings elicited by the reading

Get Writing!! Book 2 Grades 2-3   ©ECS Learning Systems, Inc., San Antonio, TX   45

Example: "Think, class, about what *Elbert's Bad Word* reminds you of. What does the book remind you of in your own life?" (I went to a party outside once. It was James' birthday, and we played all kinds of games.) "And, what does the book remind you of?" (My mother washed my mouth out with soap once because I said a bad word. The soap was gross.) "That's a pretty hard reminder, isn't it?" (Yeah.)

"Now I want you to write about what the story reminds you of. What do you think about from your own life when you hear the story of Elbert? When you are finished with your reader response, put it in the red box."

4. **On another day, talk with the children about how the story made them feel.**

Example: This exercise can extend many children's vocabularies, not only by listing and discussing words, but also by categorizing words that have similar meanings. Explore feelings associated with being at a party, having something happen that makes people say bad words, being punished for saying bad words, or being taught bad words to say. If you record the "feeling" words they offer, the class will have a bank of vocabulary words from which to choose when they write.

5. **Ask children to write about feelings they associate with the story.** Put some or all of the papers on the board. There will eventually be a whole bulletin board filled with writings about the story.

Cue

What did you notice about the reading? What did the reading remind you of? How did the reading make you feel?

 Daily Writing Activities

In the following prompts, you will want to substitute the appropriate term for the words *story*, *book*, and *piece*. Children may be reading poems, stories, fables, books, or folktales; use whichever applies at the moment.

1. Who do you think was the most important character in the story or book?

2. Is there a character in the story or book who is at all like you?

3. Think about the place where the story is set. Do you know any place like that? Does the setting of the story remind you of anywhere you have been?

4. Did you notice that your feelings about the reading changed as you read further and further in the story or book?

5. Do you think the title of this piece is a good one? If you don't think so, write why not, and also write an example of what might have been a good title.

6. Think about whether or not you liked the piece. Write about why you did or did not like it.

7. What would you say to a friend who asked you about the piece you just read? Should he or she read this piece? Be sure to explain why or why not.

8. What picture or image comes to your mind when you think about what you just read?

9. Was there anything in the piece that confused you?

10. Draw a picture in your mind of the setting of the story. Now write a description of the picture in your mind.

11. Before you started reading, what did you think the piece would be about? Were you right?

12. What was the best part of the piece you just read? What was your least favorite part of the piece?

13. What is there about the piece that makes you want to read more by the author? What is there in the piece that makes you not want to read more by the author?

14. Did you enjoy reading this piece? What did you especially like? What did you dislike?

15. Does this piece make you think of something else you have read? Write about the two pieces and how they are alike and different.

16. If the author of the piece were in the classroom, what would you ask him/her?

17. What was there about the piece that made you want to keep reading? What was there about how the piece was written that made you want to keep reading?

18. What did the author do to make the piece likeable? What could the author have done to make it better?

19. If the author were in this room right now, what could you say about how to make the piece better?

20. If you were a parent right now, what would you want your son or daughter to notice about the piece you just read?

Get Writing!!

 Across the Curriculum

The idea of responding to literature is not new, although the kinds of responses in this lesson are not found in traditional language arts and literature classes. Outside the area of literature, the idea of responding to the material in textbooks is almost nonexistent. The reading task in science, for example, is to find information and write it on the test paper or use it in the laboratory.

For instance, a section about simple machines in the science text is about the inclined plane. Using the principles of responding to literature, you might follow the reading with a question like, "What do you think is the most important idea in the section about the inclined plane?" and write the ideas on the board as they occur.

List the variety of ideas readers think are most important in the reading. As a next step, get a group consensus about how the list can be ranked.

Example: "If the author who wrote the part about inclined planes were in our room right now, what would you ask?" [Write the questions on the board.] "What was there about the section that confused you?" [Make a list on the board.]

"Is there anything in your memory about an inclined plane? Have you ever used an inclined plane to help lift something, and didn't even know what it was called?" (Yeah, but not me. The guy who mows the lawns on our street uses a ramp from the street to his truck bed to get the mowers on and off. It looks like an inclined plane.) [Direct students to write a small section of the text in their own words in a way that will clarify one of the confusions on the board.]

©ECS Learning Systems, Inc., San Antonio, TX

On another occasion, students can write to the author of a book and ask how to clarify a confusing section. Several students could collaborate on a script with the author and a student in conversation to get the author to explain inclined planes, for example, in a way that is not confusing.

Textbooks often pose a special reading problem for learners. By using the **Writing About Reading** activity, you can promote a different sort of reading, a more attentive reading, and a subsequent discussion and writing that can enhance the quality of learning from subject matter texts.

©ECS Learning Systems, Inc., San Antonio, TX

 English Language Learners

There is a vast difference between talking on the playground or in the street and talking in the classroom about academic vocabulary and text material.

In the classroom, it is often helpful to use the second language as a tool for comprehension. It isn't the first or second reading of textual material that causes students to construct an idea or concept in science; it is the amount of conversation about the idea that supports understanding. Writing and reading prompts elaborate on the whole-language combination to make sense out of text.

Consider a social studies chapter about westward movement in the United States. Aside from the necessity of providing as much information as possible before the reading, it is helpful for children to take the material in relatively small pieces. Begin by reading a paragraph silently. Then ask students what they noticed about the main idea or main image. Write their ideas on the board. Finally, ask the children to select from the ideas on the board the one they think is most important. This idea can be recorded as a one-sentence statement of the main idea of the paragraph.

Taking one paragraph at a time is quite tedious, so move into larger pieces of text quickly. Follow up with conversation and writing about the main ideas. The reading takes longer this way, but students will know more at the end of the chapter. The combination of reading, discussion, and writing in subject matter context enhances language development.

 Tip

There is one caveat to which we must all pay attention. Notice that the reading is always *silent*. If young readers are seeing the text for the first time, they should rarely read aloud. Oral reading should occur with material that has been practiced so that everyone in the classroom can hear reading done well. It does no one, reader nor listener, any good to participate in oral reading when the reader stumbles and hesitates over new print, whether it is in a reader's native language or not.

Language Activity Sheet
Writing About Reading

This is your chance to write about what you think after reading a story. In the spaces below, write sentences that answer the questions.

1. Before you began reading, what did you think the story would be about?

    _____

    _____

2. Now that you have read the story, what are two things you noticed?

    _____

    _____

3. Now that you have had a chance to read and think about the story, what do you think is the best way to tell what it is about?

    _____

    _____

4. When we read stories, there are often things that remind us of our own lives and people we know. What was there in the story that reminded you of something in your own life?

    _____

    _____

5. What was your favorite part of the story? Write a sentence below that tells about your favorite part.

_____

_____

6. What was there about the story, or even about how the author wrote, that made you want to keep reading?

_____

_____

7. How would you describe the story to a friend?

_____

_____

6 Writing a Story: Character

—*Typically, story writers tend to write to one of two emphases, character or plot.*

Information for the Teacher

Writing a Story: Character is the first of several activities in this book that feature a way of looking at story writing. First, we take the point of view that stories have elements in a pattern. **Character**, **setting**, **problem**, and **resolution** appear in all stories in some form. To become good at writing stories, young writers need to learn to work with these four elements.

Some writers invent characters and write a story that features those character(s). Other writers already have a plot in mind and develop characters to carry it. **Writing a Story: Character** helps children learn how to build one or more characters, and then write a story in which the character(s) play roles.

There is nothing in this or subsequent lessons to suggest that any young writer should be "forced" into writing from character or plot. There is no reason to believe that one approach is "better" than the other, or easier. Writers just use two different approaches, and young writers need to learn them both.

There is also nothing in this lesson to suggest that to write on the basis of character means the character must be fully developed before the story begins. In fact, this is rare, as the story itself routinely provides the framework for character development. But writers who write to character often have a basic **character** idea before they begin, and use their writing as a search for a story for this character.

Objective

Young writers will compose a story, or at least a story beginning, on the basis of one or more characters of their own creation.

 ## Conducting the Lesson

1. **While standing at the overhead projector or the board, explain that one of the ways to write a story is to begin with a character, and then write what the character tells us to write. Write the name and age of your character on the board.**

   Example: "So I am going to begin a story right here at the board. But I need a character first. I think my character will be named Danielle. [Write the character's name on a corner of the board.] I think she will be seven years old. [Write the character's age below her name.] Oh, and I think she lives in Wyoming." [Write the state below the name and age.]

   Practice this procedure several times before doing it for the first time with children; not so you have a script ready, but so you will have confidence in the procedure. This process is a risk. It requires that the teacher write the first part or more of a story in front of the children. There are two reasons for this. One, young writers need to see writing going on right before their eyes. And two, young writers need to learn to trust the writing itself to promote the story.

2. **Write the first sentence about the character on the board.**

   Example: Danielle rubbed her sleepy eyes awake.

3. **Write a second sentence on the board.**

   Example: "I need to let my readers know more about Danielle. I think I will put something about her age in the second sentence: **Just like the other children in her class, Danielle just became seven years old.**"

4. **Write one or two more sentences, then ask the students to tell you what they can tell about the character from reading.**

   Example: [It was Tuesday, and there would be a party today in her second grade. Hers would be the third birthday party of the year in Mrs. Brumley's class.] "I want to hear from you, about Danielle. Who is she? What do you know about her?" (She's in second grade.) (It's her birthday.) (She's seven years old today.) (Her teacher's name is Mrs. Brumley.) (It's Tuesday.)

   Invent a character and write a story around him - her - it.

"Do you think the first paragraph is finished? What do you think?" (Yeah, I think it's finished.) "Well then, what happens next?" (Danielle gets out of bed and has breakfast.) "Why? Why do I have to tell about getting out of bed and having breakfast?" (Because that's what happens next. After you wake up, you always get out of bed and have your breakfast.) "Sure, that's what people do every day, but do I have to say it? Look at this:

> **When she met the children at her mailbox in front of her house, everyone said, 'Happy Birthday.' They were very excited as they walked to school together**.

"There, I got her out of the house without ... well, wait a minute. Did she ever get out of bed and have her breakfast?" (Of course, she's walking to school already.) "But I didn't say she got out of bed and ate breakfast. How do you know, if the writer didn't say it?" (You just know. She has to get out of bed if she's walking to school.) "Sure. Of course you're right. What you're saying is, as the writer, I don't have to write everything my character does. Some of these things we just know, don't we?"

5. **Ask the students to take a piece of paper from their writing folders and prepare to write a sentence that begins a story about a character.** Pause for 30 seconds, then give them 10 seconds to write the character's name in the upper left-hand corner. Pause again, then give them 5 seconds to write the character's age under the name.

6. **In one minute or so, call time.** If most of those engaged are finished in one minute, leave several more seconds for most of those left. Then say something like, "If you aren't finished with your sentence, keep working so you can finish before we move on."

Tip

While there will be several in every class who don't begin right away, most of the young writers will begin to write immediately, without asking how to spell this word or that.

Focusing on "most" does not mean the "few" are not important, but that the activity is working. Carry on as long as "most" are engaged. Help the "few" as little as you can get away with, urging as much independence as they can handle.

7. **Listen to a few sentences, then ask them to write their next sentence.**

   Example: "We will need to know something about your character, so remember that as you write the next sentence." After another minute, say, "If you can think of the third sentence, just go right on and write it."

> Several of the children will get "hooked" by their character. Don't stop them, and don't direct them further. They'll keep writing until the flow runs out. Lead the rest through the beginning of the story, sentence by sentence, until they have four or five sentences. The procedures to this point will have consumed approximately ten minutes. That's enough in the second grade.

8. **The next day, maybe two or more days later, conduct a similar activity.** Begin by writing sentences on the board. Write your own first several sentences on the board, then turn it over to the children, just as described above. Give them several minutes to work, leading some and allowing space for those who are working well on their own. At a good place in the period, direct them to find a place to stop and put their papers in their folder.

9. **The following week, repeat the activity, with either a new story or one of the story-beginnings from last week.** Give them a specific amount of time to work on the activity. Tell the children they are free to work on their stories whenever they have time, but there will also be a formal writing time each day. Give them a story beginning two or three times each week for several weeks. This will give them lots of starters in their folder, just as practicing writers have. The purpose is to have several pieces of writing in progress all the time. This will give them enough material for several months.

> This is but one story-writing strategy. If it does not engage everyone in the room, try to encourage the students to do it, even though it might not "feel" natural. As they become familiar with more and more ways to handle their writing, they will become better writers. This is but one way to handle stories.

    57

Writing a Story: Character

 ## Daily Writing Activities

For this lesson, there are no daily activities, in the sense of a series of tasks or cues. Over a period of several months, you may use the lesson as many as 15 to 20 times, but you will always need to invent your own beginning. The children will then write to the set of information you use. There are, however, various ways to set up the beginnings:

1. Character's Name - Age - Home Town

2. Character's Name - Grade in School - Home State

3. Character's Name - Time of Day (Morning, Night, and so forth)

4. Character's Name - Weather (Rain, Wind, and so forth) - Time of Day

5. Character's Name - Second Character's Name - Kind of Animal

It is clear from the idea sets above that there are few limitations on the kinds of items that will work. One constant of each set is a character. In the primary grades, and in the earlier stages of the activity at any grade level, the use of a name is helpful, but after a while, introduce different kinds of characters. For example, an idea set might include "A Calico Cat - Early Morning - Winter."

These idea sets are not story starters, because the writer actually starts the story. In writing stories, the creativity is in the start, the act of inventing the character and the character's direction.

 ## Across the Curriculum

What would happen if the idea set contained a character's name (Benjamin Franklin), weather (rain storm), and time of day (night)? In the absence of prior knowledge, the answer is nothing. However, if they read about the character in their social studies program and had some background, students could use the idea set to write a story.

There are all kinds of people, or characters, with whom second- and third-graders need to become familiar. If they can learn about Franklin, Washington, and Lincoln, they can certainly learn about Chief Joseph, Seneca, and Pontiac; or WEB DuBois, Frederick Douglass, and Marcus Garvey; or Florence Nightengale, Marie Curie, and Dolly Madison. The biographical focus can change with the month, the week, even the day. Every biography provides background, and every piece of background is grist for the story writing mill.

 ## English Language Learners

School is appealing for children and promotes their effectiveness when the school environment—expectations, morality, social routines, and so forth—reflects their comfort zones. This provides the opportunity for children to work within what they know. Some will respond and some won't. But you will provide them the freedom to respond. The rest is up to the children.

Everyone brings "who they are," their experiences and passions, to school with them. Use this in **Writing a Story: Character**. For example:

1. "The character I am going to use today is named Mai Lei. Her home town is San Francisco, and she is in the third grade."

2. "My character is Rosalia. She lives in New York. She rides a bus every day to school."

3. "My character today is Anslem Begay. He lives in Lower Greasewood and watches the family sheep every afternoon after school."

The basic elements of stories are culture-free. All peoples write, read, tell, and listen to stories. The story is within the range of every child in school.

 ©ECS Learning Systems, Inc., San Antonio, TX

Writing a Story: Character

Character: _____

Age: _____

Home Town: _____

1. Write a first sentence for a story. Include the character's name in the first sentence.

_____

_____

2. Write the next sentence. Make sure the reader learns something about your character.

_____

_____

3. Write the next sentence in your story. Make sure your reader knows either your character's age or home town by the end of the third sentence.

_____

_____

_____

60   Get Writing!! Book 2 Grades 2-3   ©ECS Learning Systems, Inc., San Antonio, TX

4. Write the fourth sentence in your story.

_____

5. Read the sentences you have written so far. In the spaces below, write what you think your story might be about. It is about more than your character. What do you think is going to happen to your character?

_____

_____

6. Write a sentence that tells what you think might happen to your character.

_____

_____

7. If you know what you want to write next in your story, begin writing below and write as much as you can. When you run out of room to write, write some more on a separate sheet of paper.

_____

_____

_____

_____

7 Writing a Story: Setting

—Stories happen somewhere—in forests, at bends in the river, in office buildings, on city streets, in small towns, at seashores, in tree houses, even in prison cells.

Information for the Teacher

The setting of a story can be its focal point. While most stories tend to be either plot-driven or character-driven, setting-driven stories are not unheard of. "The Tree House" by Lois Lowry (*The Big Book for Peace*, Dutton, 1990), for instance, is a setting-driven story about two girls and their move from selfishness to cooperation and friendship. The characters are well-drawn and interesting, but the setting, two tree houses, is the focus of the story.

Focusing on setting is useful for young writers. They can take themselves to a place they have been, a favorite vacation place, a place they have studied and find interesting, or a place they have imagined completely. They can use that place as a stage to play out ideas for plot. They can people their plot with characters invented for that purpose. However, setting-driven story writing is not only for children who can't find their way with characters or plot. World-class writers use attributes of setting as their focus.

Critical to using setting to anchor the story is the writer's ability to capture the readers. The setting must be so finely drawn, so expertly described, that readers are there, feeling the rain fall on their head, seeing the hair stand up on their forearms from the sudden chill rushing across the hills. This may be over-drawn for second- and third-graders, but it is something they can work toward. This activity is about giving young writers the leadership they need to do just that.

Objective

Young writers will write stories focused on setting. They will develop their setting as a place in which characters can play out a plot. They will practice the development of setting, using whichever literary devices they need to make their setting come alive.

 ©ECS Learning Systems, Inc., San Antonio, TX

 ## Conducting the Lesson

1. **Introduce this activity using the cue below.** Ask the students to imagine a place. Pause while they are thinking, then ask them specific questions about their place. Pause again. They cannot consider all your questions, and it isn't necessary that they do. They merely need some time to ponder a question or two.

   Example: "I want you to think about a room. It can be any room, but it can't be one in your house. It can even be a room you invent, a room where you have never been, but one you might be able to draw in your head. Try to see the room in your head now. Are there windows? What do the windows look like? Is there very much light from the sun? Is it daytime, or is it night? Is there carpet on the floor, or bare wood, or maybe even cement? Is it cold, warm, hot?"

2. **Assemble the students into small groups and ask for one or two volunteers to share descriptions of their rooms.** After listening to the descriptions, send everyone to their seats to write about the room they have in their head. Instruct them to write as much as they can, as well as they can, about their room. Remind them that the room will be the setting for the story they are to think about later.

3. **After the children finish writing, engage them in a conversation about developing a story around setting.** There should follow several similar conversations about prospective characters in the rooms and the sorts of problems those characters might have to face. These are idea conversations to help young writers understand that if they begin with an interesting setting, they can put characters in it and find a story.

Think of a place where you have been, a place you know about, and find both character(s) and plot for that setting.

Writing a Story: Setting

Example: "Bring your writing with you to the rug and let's talk about your room. What happens in there? What kind of room is it?" (It's like a kitchen.) **"Well, what happens in that room?" (They make food and eat in there.)** (It's a family, and it's their house.) "How many? Tell me about the family." (It's a mother and father and three kids and a dog and cat.) "Do the pets live in the house, or are they outside?" (They're in the house.) "Do they chew up the furniture? Are they both house-broken?" (The cat is, but the dog makes mistakes sometimes.)

"It seems there is a problem the family has to solve. What do you think they'll do about it? Whose dog is it, anyway?" (It's the father's dog. He will have to teach the dog not to make mistakes.)

4. **Remind the students of the elements of stories.**

   Example: "Stories have characters, settings, problems, and solutions. You already have a setting and characters, the dog and the father. The problem they have to solve is to teach the dog better. All you have to do is find a solution, and you have the story worked out. Now go to your seats and begin to put the characters and the problem into your room. Try it and see what happens."

5. **As with story writing from character development (see Writing a Story: Character p. 54), the objective here is to create story-beginnings.** We want the children to invent many settings, explore them, describe them in as much detail as they can muster, put characters in them, and then make the characters do something that fits the setting.

6. **Students should seek to complete two stories each month for reading aloud in writers' workshop, for revision, and for subsequent publishing.** Remind them that they already have several story beginnings based on characters in their portfolio. In time, they may have two dozen or more beginnings they can go back to during the year.

Characters often define a plot. Sometimes the setting itself will define a plot. Providing "story starters" can be an effective way to promote story writing, but most of the time the creativity is in the development of the *story beginning*. Fundamental creativity is preempted when someone other than the writer dictates the beginning. Beginnings are the root of creativity in story writing.

©ECS Learning Systems, Inc., San Antonio, TX

 Daily Writing Activities

As with **Writing a Story: Character**, there are no daily activities for **Writing a Story: Setting**. But there are several ideas for carrying out the procedures in the context of young writers' creative instincts. Below are some catalysts for thinking about setting:

1. Think about settings as buildings and/or rooms, hallways, cafeterias, meeting rooms, places to eat or prepare food, places to sleep, places to watch television, large rooms in which people can watch movies or dance, tiny rooms with mice, workshops, and rooms with fireplaces.

2. Think of settings as places near the edge of the forest, alongside the great wheatfields of Kansas or Nebraska or North Dakota, or beside a stormy sea in Maine or Washington.

3. Suggest young writers "see" the streets of a big city, the narrow roads through the central square of a small town, or the empty stretches of blacktop through rural Missouri. Of course, if the second- and third-graders live in Cedar Falls, Iowa, it might not make sense to try their creativity with the coast of Oregon, but every community, every neighborhood, every town and city, every rural township has places with which the children are familiar and around which they can weave a story.

4. There are stories set in trees, in gardens, in shoes. One of the more interesting activities for young children is a fluency exercise about where stories can take place. Talk with the class a moment about settings as places where stories take place. Give them some examples [*Two Bad Ants* (Van Allsburg, Houghton Mifflin Co., 1988) and *The Great Kapok Tree* (Cherry, Harcourt Brace, 1990), for instance], and ask that they think of settings. As they call out ideas, write them on the board. Organize the list. Suggest someone start a story from category one, someone else from category two, and so forth.

Tip

Remember, no activity will strike all young writers in the same manner. It is not only possible, but probable, that this story-writing activity will leave some young writers cold. That is why there are so many other story-writing activities in this book.

Writing a Story: Setting

 ## Across the Curriculum

Consider the connection between social studies and story writing based on setting description. In a unit on transportation, the setting of a story might be a railroad car traveling across Texas. A whole body of information must be included in the setting description to "force" the children to internalize what they are learning about rail transportation.

In every social studies program there is a study of the state in which the children reside. The setting of a story might be Huntsville, Alabama, and the plot may have something to do with the space camp and an accident on the river. The story is fiction, of course, but the setting is accurate. To write the setting accurately, the children must use the information from their social studies program as the anchor of their stories.

English Language Learners

A major difficulty faced by children whose native language is not English is the "affective filter" through which school content and daily operations must flow. If the filter is dense, a limited amount of content and school operations get through.

If young writers are working on what they know, the affective filter is reduced. Given the opportunity to establish a story setting based on their own experience or imagination, they are free of the barriers that come from unfamiliarity with background information.

For example, as two young writers begin stories about immigration from entirely different perspectives, one writes about a small boat in a violent sea. The other creates a story setting about walking from a Central American country. Both children, working in their native language, write enthusiastically. The children have something to write about, something to say, and the story, with room for their own version of setting, is their vehicle.

It is not necessary to make an issue out of experiential differences in the classroom when teaching a setting-driven conception of story. If the activity is conducted as described, young writers will know they can work from their strengths, from what they know.

Language Activity Sheet

Writing a Story: Setting

1. Think of a place where you have been that you have good memories about. Write the name of the place or a short description in the space below.

____

2. Make a list of words or phrases you could use to describe the sounds someone might hear in the place you named above.

__________ __________ __________ __________

__________ __________ __________ __________

3. Write the colors someone might find in the place where you have good memories.

__________ __________ __________ __________

4. Write a sentence that tells something about this place where you have been. Be sure to include something about the sounds you might hear there.

____

____

5. Write a sentence about one of the good memories you have about this place.

____

____

6. Make a list of things someone might see in this place.

_____   _____

_____   _____

_____   _____

7. Think about that place very carefully. Who might be there?

_____

8. This is a place to start a story. Begin with something about the place you have been
writing about so far. Then introduce a character. (Use the other side of this page if
you need more space.)

_____

_____

_____

_____

Writing the Common Story

—The matter of curiosity is at the center of story writing. Curiosity means asking: What if ...? What would happen if ...? How could it be made to work?

Information for the Teacher

A common story is one written on the basis of another, but from a different character's point of view. For example, in Jon Scieszka's *The True Story of the Three Little Pigs* (Viking, 1989), the pigs aren't nice, but the wolf is.

The psychology of attention indicates that human beings cannot concentrate on more than one piece of unpracticed stimulation at a time. Story writing demands attention to character, setting, problem, resolution, coherence, and all of the intricacies of literacy at once. In this activity, characters, setting, and plot are essentially provided in the original story. The only requirements of the young writer are the curiosity to generate a different view and sufficient attention to literacy to make the story "work."

In **Writing the Common Story**, young writers speculate about a change of perspective—What would happen if Jack in *Jack and the Beanstalk* were breaking and entering the giant's home, if the third billy goat in *The Three Billy Goats Gruff* challenged the troll to a fight, or if the girl with the golden locks broke into the Three Bears' house?

Objective

Young writers will speculate on how a different character's view will change a story, and they will write that alternative view as a story. In this lesson, a "story" will be essentially a plot outline for most of the children. Some will "flesh out" their plot outlines, but thinking and the outline are the only real requirements for the activity.

This activity is about the mental discipline required to follow a line of reasoning to a conclusion. Young children can do this, but we have to give them the opportunity—and teach them.

Get Writing!! Book 2 Grades 2-3 ©ECS Learning Systems, Inc., San Antonio, TX

 ## Conducting the Lesson

1. **Read *The True Story of the Three Little Pigs*. Ask the students to describe any differences they notice between this story and other stories of the three little pigs.**

   Example: "What did you notice in the story?" (It was about the three little pigs, but the pigs were bad, not the wolf.) "Oh, you noticed that?" (Yeah, and the wolf was good in the story.) "Yes, he seemed to be good." (And the pigs were mean.) "Do you think pigs are mean?" (No.) "But you said they were in the story." (Yes, but it's only a story.)

2. **Introduce to the class the idea that the wolf in *Little Red Riding Hood* is good instead of bad.** Ask them to share their ideas about how that would change the story.

   Example: "If the wolf were good, he wouldn't want to eat the little girl." (And the wolf wouldn't go to the grandmother and get in her bed.) "Maybe the grandmother let the wolf in so she could teach the girl a lesson. Maybe the grandmother and the wolf were friends." (*Laughter*) "They did live in the forest, you know." (Yeah, maybe they were friends, and the grandmother told the wolf to scare Little Red Riding Hood so she wouldn't be in the woods alone any more.) "Maybe, indeed. Maybe that's what happened."

3. **Remind the students of the story *The Three Billy Goats Gruff*.** Pose a scenario that compares the story to real life.

   Example: "What would happen if you were sitting in your living room watching a football game, and a stranger came in your front door and walked through the room toward the back door? Wouldn't your mother or father want to know what's going on?" (Yeah.) "Well, suppose another stranger came in and when your mother asked what was going on, the stranger said not to worry because someone else was coming in later. So when the third stranger came in, he hurt your father. Isn't that what happened in *The Three Billy Goats Gruff*?" (Yeah, except that the bridge wasn't the troll's house.) "Maybe it was. Maybe since the troll lives under the bridge, he calls it his house."

Think of a story you know very well. Think of who the hero or heroine is. Think of a way to rewrite the story to make a different hero or heroine.

Writing the Common Story

4. **Ask the students to think of a story they know, perhaps a story they remember from when they were much younger.** They must know the story and everyone in it. Most children will come up with something. Of those who do not, most will be part of the conversation, but it might be an hour or so, maybe a day or two, before they can remember a story.

5. **Gather several children together into a small group to talk about their story and more about common stories.** Select the group on the basis that everyone will complete this project. The procedure is to "talk through" a story to help youngsters form alternative views of characters and situations.

   Example: "What story are you thinking about?" (*Jack and the Beanstalk*.) "And if your story is about *Jack and the Beanstalk*, who else could tell the story?" (The giant isn't very nice to the goose. She has to lay eggs all the time.) "So the problem in the story is that the goose is getting tired of laying eggs all the time." (Yes.)

   "Maybe Jack should talk to the giant and see if he'll let the goose visit him down at the bottom of the beanstalk." (I don't think the giant would like that, but maybe if the goose would bring him one egg a week, he'd let her go.) "You may be right. The goose could rest all week with Jack, and then lay one egg a week for the giant."

6. **Debrief:** From the initial conversation, this activity is similar to the earlier story-writing activities based on characters and settings. Begin with a small group of children, the initial Common Story Writing Group. Members of the group would compose their common stories for group sharing and eventual posting on a "Best Effort Board." As others show interest, form new groups and lead those children through their first common story.

Tip

Eventually, most of the children will be writing common stories. Some children will write two or three because of the novelty. A couple will write a dozen. Several won't write any. Those who don't write common stories can work on character- and setting-driven stories.

It is utterly irrelevant what cue or prompt causes children to write. The only relevancy necessary in the writing classroom is something that causes everyone to write something every day.

©ECS Learning Systems, Inc., San Antonio, TX

 Daily Writing Activities

Young writers do not need to write a common story every day, every week, or even every month. **Writing the Common Story** is a story-writing idea or focus, and only one of the options described in this book to keep students involved in writing.

For the purpose of having available several ways to promote the common story, consider the following possibilities:

1. There are common story ideas in all of the fairy tales most of us learn early in our lives.

    Example: The spider in *Little Miss Muffet* was only trying to be friendly; and although no one knew it at the time, Humpty Dumpty was climbing the wall so he could pick some flowers for his mother from the lawn on the other side.

2. Much of the literature children read can be rendered into common stories.

    Example: In E.B. White's *Charlotte's Web* (Harper Trophy, 1999), it may not have been the fact that Wilber was the runt of the litter that made him a candidate for pork chops. It might have been that he had spent most of his youth making life miserable for the farmer by getting out of his pen and rooting up the garden, and the farmer was tired of it.

3. There is also an "alternative history."

    Example: Second- and third-graders learn about Pilgrims around the fall of the year. What if the celebration had been started in March? What if the indigenous people had never shared their knowledge of planting with the Pilgrims?

 ## Across the Curriculum

The common story is an excellent opportunity to truly master social studies material. An application of knowledge to alternative history requires students know well the history under scrutiny, as well as the history of an alternative time period.

Suppose, for instance, Columbus landed in the new world in the late 1800s, rather than the 1400s. How might that have changed American history? How might that have changed the indigenous peoples in what was to become the United States?

Suppose while working as a surveyor, George Washington did not survive a fall into a ravine. Who might have been the "Father of Our Country"? Who might have been the Revolutionary War General? This lesson calls for research about who was living at the time and the influence various leaders had. It requires that students speculate (ponder/wonder) about what it means to be the "Father of Our Country" and what it takes to be a Revolutionary War leader.

Are such questions and pursuits too strenuous for second- and third-graders? Of course not! Their attention to and knowledge of television heros and heroines indicates they have every capability necessary to speculate on history from this perspective.

 English Language Learners

Young people from scores of countries and cultures attend our schools today. Collectively, in a large school district as many as 50 to 60 different languages may be spoken. A "half-full" perspective of this reality is that many more stories are available from which everyone can learn and gather inspiration for writing common stories of their own.

Example: "This evening I want everyone to explain to the adults at home what we were doing in school today with the common story. Explain that we thought about how stories might seem different if they were told through different characters' eyes. I want you to see if your uncles or grandmothers or mothers and fathers can suggest ways to think about the stories like we have been doing here in school. We'll talk about your stories tomorrow."

It has long been thought that no matter how much attention the school system pays to the variety of cultures and languages represented in our classrooms, the message remains that it is to move toward some sort of homogeneous American culture and English language. Use what children have at home and in the neighborhood as valued content for legitimate learning, and the school system will become a less alien place.

Get Writing!! Book 2 Grades 2-3   ©ECS Learning Systems, Inc., San Antonio, TX   75

Language Activity Sheet
Writing the Common Story

1. Think of a story you know very well. Write its name or the title of the story in the space.

   _____

2. Write the name of the main character in the "Main Character" space, and write the names of other characters in the spaces with numbers in front of them.

   _____   a. _____   b. _____
   Main Character

   c. _____   d. _____

3. If you were telling a friend who had never heard the story about where the story took place (the setting of the story) what would you say? Write in one or more sentences what you would tell your friend.

   _____

   _____

4. Think very carefully now. What is the story about? Think of a way to tell what the story is about in two full sentences.

   _____

   _____

   _____

5. Now you have to think very carefully again. Think about how the story would change if the character in space number two were the main character. Make your character number two the main character, and write in the space below how the story would have to be changed.

_____

_____

_____

6. Suppose your character in space number three were to be the main character. How would the story have to be changed? Write how the story would change in full sentences below.

_____

_____

_____

7. On a separate piece of paper, or on the back of this page, write the story with your character number one as the main character.

9 Descriptions and Explanations

—Nearly everything we will ever write is a description or an explanation.

 ## Information for the Teacher

When we write stories, we describe characters, settings, problems, and resolutions. We explain our recent experiences to friends and relatives in letters and explain our feelings in diaries. In reports, we explain or describe what we have seen or read, and in poetry, we explain or describe feelings, images, and ideas. In autobiographical pieces, we explain and describe our lives.

In this lesson, young writers will begin to learn how to give readers a peek into what the writer knows, what the writer "sees," and how the writer senses things. They will begin to think of the connection between reader and writer. This is the start of writing like a reader, of seeing what a reader sees. The writing must paint an image or idea. It's effectiveness is evaluated by how thoroughly the reader understands the writer's description or explanation.

To do this, young writers need to learn the following:

- Descriptions and explanations are specific and clear. A reader should be able to see, hear, or feel exactly what the writer saw, heard, or felt.

- Descriptions and explanations are sometimes figurative. (While it isn't necessary to use literary terminology with second- or third-graders, they certainly can use similes, maybe even a metaphor or two, in their writing.)

- Descriptions and explanations can appear in any kind of writing.

 ## Objective

Young writers will write short descriptions and explanations that are progressively clearer and more precise. They will begin to see writing as a way to introduce readers to the writer's vision; the writer's sense of what things are, how things work, and what things look like. As a part of this process, the young writer will be exposed to the matter of whether or not his/her writing works.

Here, young writers need an audience beyond the teacher. They must read their writings aloud for the class (and later in smaller groups), and receive feedback (not criticism) about whether their pieces work and why.

Feedback must come as reflections. (I can see the colors in the flower…. I got confused when you started writing about when to subtract…. I didn't understand what you wrote about when she lived….) Feedback will not label the writing as "good" or "bad," but rather, tell writers if their objective is accomplished. After a reading, ask the class, "What did you notice? What did you see? What did you hear?" If the writer agrees with their responses, the writing works. If the writing doesn't work, the reader's feedback tells how and what to rethink and possibly revise.

Tip

With respect to public readings:

- Writers never tell the audience about a writing before they begin reading aloud

- The writer does not introduce the work; the writing must stand on its own

- The writer never defends his/her writing to the class

Get Writing!! Book 2 Grades 2-3   ©ECS Learning Systems, Inc., San Antonio, TX   79

Descriptions and Explanations

 ## Conducting the Lesson

1. **Initiate a class discusson about description.**

   Example: "We all know what pizza is, don't we?" (Yes.) "Well now, if you had to describe pizza to someone who had never seen one, what would you say? Remember, you are only describing what pizza looks like." (It's round and has cheese on it.) "Round?" (Sometimes it's square.) "Yes it is. Sometimes it's square, and sometimes it's round, so how would we describe what it looks like so someone who has never seen it would recognize it?"

2. **In response to a cue, make a list of students' descriptive phrases and a list of comments on the board.**

3. **Point to the list of descriptions and ask students to use one of the items in a sentence.**

   Example: "Someone give me a sentence that contains one of the items on the list." (**Pizza is a kind of dinner you get in Italian restaurants. It is red from the sauce and yellow from the cheese.**) "Well, what do we know from these two sentences?" (It's red and yellow. You eat it for dinner.) "Is that all?" (No. She said you get it in Italian restaurants, but we get ours from the grocery store and cook it at home.) "So the colors describe pizza, and explain that it's a dinner food?" (Yeah.)

   "How about another sentence from our list." (**It's round and sometimes square.**) "Another sentence." (**When you cut the round kind, your piece is like a triangle.**) "Another?" (The crust.) "What about the crust?" (**Crust is around the pizza, like a border or a fence around it.**)

 *Cue*

Write as much as you can as well as you can about a rose. Try to describe a rose so someone who has never seen one can picture it after reading your piece.

4. **As the children give their sentences, write them on the board.** Read the sentences aloud, and solicit readers from the group. When all the listed items have been put into sentences, seek a larger piece of descriptive writing. Write this description on the board.

   Example: "Now boys and girls, let's see if we can write a description of pizza. Who can use the sentences on the board to write a larger piece that will describe pizza?" "Start with *pizza* so we know what you are writing about." (**Pizza is a food that is round and sometimes square. It is red from the sauce and yellow from the cheese. You cut it in a lot of pieces, and the pieces of the round pizza look like triangles.**)

5. **On another day, or at a different time during the same day, solicit from each young writer a description, this time not limited to the ideas and sentences on the board.** Ask them to write their descriptions on their papers. The rule is to write as clearly as possible so identification can occur solely by their description. Ask students to share their writings by reading them aloud. As described earlier in this lesson, incorporate feedback into the sharing.

6. **On another day, conduct a similar activity focusing on aroma.** The question is to describe something on the basis of its smell(s), and the procedure is similar to that above with respect to sight. As applicable, follow this with a session on taste(s) and then a session on sound(s). Over several days, students will produce lists of ideas and sentences for posting in the Writing Center. Call attention to the variety of ways things can be described.

7. **When everything has been posted and reviewed, set up an activity for audience feedback.**

   Example: "Class, this is your chance to write a description of pizza that other people will read. I want you to read the writings we've posted about pizza in the Writing Center. I also want you to use as much as you think you need from the board and whatever else you think of to write the best description of pizza you can. Then we will give your papers to the fifth-graders to read and decide whose papers best describe pizza.

8. **Prepare the fifth-graders for the judging by telling them to score papers either with a 1 (Very Good Description), 2 (Pretty Good Description), or 3 (Needs Some More Work), and to write on the paper exactly why they scored the paper as they did.** Remind the second- or third-graders that their descriptions to the other people have to be detailed. Also tell them that when they get their papers back from the fifth-graders, they will use the comments as ideas and directions for revision. (**Note:** Make sure to code their papers so the writers remain anonymous.)

Descriptions and Explanations

 ## Daily Writing Activities

The following writing ideas are merely prompts. You can select various applications of the procedures described in this lesson. Any one activity could be explored in a single day or over several days and culminate in a writing session.

1. Describe lasagna or tacos or piki bread or bacon and eggs or spaghetti.

2. Describe a hyacinth or a rose or a violet or a tulip.

3. Describe one of your friends, a pet, a car you ride in, or the kitchen in your house.

4. Describe what a chocolate bar tastes like. Describe the inside of a tomato. Describe what toast smells like. Describe what an ice cube feels like.

5. Describe what it feels like to be cold in the winter. Describe what it feels like when you are thirsty.

6. Explain how to add 15 and 6. (**Note to the Teacher:** The initial instructional stage for writing explanations might be writing directions, such as asking students to write directions for adding 15 and 6, like the following: "You can add six beans, Unifix Cubes, or dots on the paper to 15 and count the total. You can add five and six and carry the one ten which you then add to the other ten to make two tens and a one, or 21." On the basis of the directions, young writers can begin to think about explanations.)

7. Write an explanation for how to identify a square.

8. Write directions for drawing a square or a triangle or a parallelogram, then explain one or more of those geometric shapes.

9. Explain who Benjamin Franklin is. Explain what Thanksgiving is about.

10. Explain what your mother, father, sister, aunt, or grandfather does for a living.

11. Explain what an attorney does. Explain what a veteranarian does, a cardiologist, a cartographer, a civil engineer, and so forth.

 ## Across the Curriculum

There are several cross-curricular applications represented in the daily activities. Consider the field of biographical study for the cross-curricular application.

Suppose you make available in the classroom several biographical collections, [e.g., *Indian Chiefs*, by Russell Freedman (Scholastic, 1987); *Lives of the Musicians*, by Kathleen Krull and Kathryn Hewitt (Harcourt Brace, 1993); *Lives of the Writers*, by Kathleen Krull and Kathryn Hewitt (Harcourt Brace, 1994); *Women Who Change Things*, by Linda Peavy (Scribner, 1988).] The task is for students to learn about someone, write a description of the person's importance, and explain what made the person famous enough to appear in the book.

On a day known well in advance, each student makes a short oral report to the class and posts his/her description and explanation on the Biography Board. If each child writes and makes an oral report once each month, that will make at least nine oral and written descriptions and explanations in a year, to say nothing of the amount of information the class will accumulate by listening to and reading from each other.

In the same way, youngsters who write directions for drawing rectangles and figuring measurements will learn a fair amount about these concepts. These two applications represent one of the main purposes for writing, that is, to learn.

 ## English Language Learners

The variety of children in our classrooms today represents an enormous learning opportunity. The social studies text usually contains a section on celebrations around the world. In a single classroom one student may be able to explain what a *kachina* is; another, *kwanzaa*, and another, *quilting*.

In every classroom there are opportunities to introduce the idea of exploration into various lifestyles. One student's father may have a landscaping business. Another student may work with her parents in a dry cleaning and laundry shop. One may reshelve tapes in his uncle's video rental store. There are explanations for each of these businesses, and pride to be had in delivering the explanations.

Language Activity Sheet

Descriptions and Explanations

1. Think of your favorite toy at home. Think about what it looks like. Write a sentence about what it looks like so someone could pick it out from among several other toys. Don't use the name of the toy in your sentence.

____

____

2. Write a sentence about the size of your toy. Don't use the name of the toy in your sentence. Make sure a reader would be able to find it in a toy box just because of the way you described its size.

____

____

3. Think of one more thing you could write to describe your toy. Write it in one sentence, but don't use the name of the toy in your sentence.

____

____

4. Describe your toy in two sentences. Make the description as clear as you can. You may use the name of the toy in either the first or the second sentence. You may use one or more of the ideas you wrote in sentences one, two, and three.

____

____

5. Think of a way to tell readers what you can do with your toy. This is an explanation. Explain in one sentence what you can do when you play with or use your toy.

_____

_____

6. Write another sentence about how you play with or use your toy.

_____

_____

7. On a separate sheet of paper, write a paragraph about your favorite toy. Describe your toy in the first part of the paragraph, and explain how you use or play with it in the second part of your paragraph. Write as clearly as you can. Try to make your readers "see" your toy in their minds without using the name.

10 Writing Directions

—Writing clearly is about writing that works, that tells precisely what the writer intends to say.

Information for the Teacher

Writing directions is not a new writing activity for the early grades. Teachers have been using direction-writing for years, perhaps decades, mostly because of the enormous fun the activity produces. In late November, for instance, children all over America write directions for roasting a turkey. The purpose of this kind of writing is not to master the process of writing, but to have fun with the directions and introduce children to the need for specificity in writing directions.

This is one of the few opportunities young writers have to fully appreciate the objectivity and immediacy of audience feedback. In this activity, young writers compose short pieces which they read aloud to others who, in turn, do what the writing tells them to do. If the reader does what the writer intended, the writing works. If not, the writing doesn't work.

Objective

Young writers will compose directions for accomplishing simple tasks. Their attention will focus on using the right words for the right reasons. They will receive direct audience feedback on their writing efforts, and they will revise their work in response to the feedback.

Tip In the following procedure for writing simple directions, notice the level of detail in the instructions and the emphasis on how words affect meaning, images, and ideas.

Get Writing!! Book 2 Grades 2-3 ©ECS Learning Systems, Inc., San Antonio, TX

 Conducting the Lesson

1. **Explain to students that they will receive a single direction without any further explanation.** Using only that one direction, they are to follow it without asking questions.

   Example: "I am going to ask you to do something with your paper and pencil. I am going to tell you what it is only two times; one time so you will have a chance to put it in your heads, and again, so you have a chance to make sure you heard right the first time. Don't ask me any questions about my directions because the writing has to work without me explaining it. If you don't understand my directions, or they are confusing, just do the best you can. Are we all ready? Good. Now here is my direction: **Make a line on your paper.**"

 Several children will have serious difficulty with these directions because there is not enough specificity. It is critical that you not clarify for them, that you don't lessen the ambiguity. Things will get clearer for them as you move through the activity. For now, tell them to follow the directions as well as they can.

2. **Show the class what you wanted them to do by drawing a straight horizontal line about two inches long on the board.** The children will protest heartily. (You didn't say it had to be like that.) "No, I only read the direction to you, and you had to follow it. Andrea, didn't you make a line like mine?" (Mine is real long, but your line is short.) "Are you saying that my direction didn't work very well?" (You just didn't say it was supposed to be short.) "Would my direction be better if I said the line had to be short?" (Yeah.)

3. **Give the class a revised direction with a single new detail added.**

   Example: "Okay, here's my new and revised direction: **Make a short line on your paper.**"

   Everyone will make a short horizontal line. Make a diagonal line on the board, about two inches long, telling them, "This is the line from your revised direction." The children will protest again, but not so harshly this time. They will have figured out this is a kind of game and will begin having a good time with it. "My directions didn't work again? This is a short line, and everyone in the room has a short line. It's just that your lines aren't like mine."

 Write directions for drawing a triangle without using the name of the shape in your directions.

4. **Ask students for their suggestions for making the directions clearer and introduce a specific directional term.**

   Example: "Let's try it again. If I want a short line that goes from here to here [show left to right], what do I have to write in my direction?"

   "There's a word for the kind of line I want in my direction. But first I have to know if you can learn the word. A line that goes from side to side like this is called a horizontal line. Would you like to know why it's called horizontal? Well, when you are at the ocean, or you are looking across a big field, or even down a long street, there is a place where the sky seems to meet the earth. That is called the horizon. It goes from side to side. Anything like that is called horizontal."

   "Now, here's a new direction: **On your paper, make a horizontal line about as long as your pencil.** [Everyone will make a horizontal line and use their pencil to judge length.] That's terrific. Notice that if we use the right words, we can make our writing say exactly what we want it to say, and the audience will understand."

5. **On another day, read a new direction.** Keep in mind there will be frustration again because the children have become very sensitive to clarity and specificity. Now they're looking for it, and they'll know when it isn't there.

   Example: "Here is another direction for you to follow. Just do what the direction tells you to do: **Make a horizontal line at the middle of your paper.** Now I have another for you: **Make a short line that begins at the left end of your horizontal line.**"

   "You don't get the right information from my directions?" (No!) "Okay, you tell me what else you need." (You have to say where the line goes and how long it's supposed to be and if it's straight or not.) "Then you have to help me write that sentence."

6. **Over several weeks, or months, continue to focus on specificity in writing.** Don't be reluctant to teach using the right terms (*vertical, diagonal, perpendicular, east* and *west, upward,* and so forth). New terms introduced in context tend to be learned most easily. These words are in context.

   Also, encourage young writers to think of ways to use what they are learning about clarity when they write through the genres in language arts and in the larger curriculum. This is the sort of real writing skill that needs attention all the time in order to become an automatic part of language behavior.

 Daily Writing Activities

1. Write a direction sentence for making a vertical line.

2. Write a direction sentence for making a diagonal line which runs SE to NW.

3. Write a direction sentence for making a diagonal line which runs SW to NE.

4. Write directions for making a right angle. [This doesn't necessitate a geometry lesson any more than horizontal requires geography, astronomy, or mathematics. Merely describe what "right" means when we're talking about angles. Show several right angles on the board, describe what they are supposed to look like, and be sure to show them open in various directions. On subsequent days, or if the children understand quickly, adjust the direction to reflect position of the angle (e.g., **Make a right angle open to the left.**).]

5. Without using the name of the shape, write directions for making a triangle.

6. Without using the name of the shape, write directions for making a square.

7. Without using the name of the shape, write directions for making a parallelogram. This isn't as hard as it may appear, for it's only a rectangle or square pushed over a tad so there are four parallel lines but no right angles.

8. Write directions for drawing the layout of a baseball diamond.

9. Write directions for making the capital letter **A**.

10. Write directions that tell a reader that (s)he is in a forest during a rainstorm.

    Example: "Look at a whole bunch of trees. There are so many trees that you can't see more than 50 feet ahead. You can feel the water in the soil under your feet, and water is falling through the leaves and branches above your head."

11. Write directions that help a reader tell that (s)he is sitting in a room while someone is smoking.

12. Write directions that tell readers how to recognize a big dog loose in the neighborhood.

13. Write directions that show the reader that a hill is very steep.

14. Write directions for walking from the school building to the front door of your house.

15. Write directions for finding the name Porter, Alan in the telephone book.

16. Write directions for drawing a cat (horse, tree, dog, giraffe, car).

17. Write directions for finding the definition of *lip* in a dictionary.

18. Write directions for finding out who was the fifth President of the United States.

19. Write directions for subtracting 26 from 42.

20. Write directions for subtracting 26 from 40.

 Across the Curriculum

Activities 14 through 20 on the preceding page all suggest applications across the curriculum for using **Writing Directions**. Activity 14 is an early geography project in making maps; every set of directions is a verbal rendition of an actual map. Young writers can also write directions for finding their bedroom in their house or for navigating the garage and finding their bicycle.

Activities 15, 17, and 18 direct young writers to reference materials and make them think carefully about procedures for using them.

One of the best early applications of writing in mathematics is procedural. Certainly there are all sorts of understandings associated with mathematical knowledge, and procedures are only one set. But procedures are not irrelevant. In addition, when young writers, or young mathematicians for that matter, have to grapple with the specifics of procedures, they increase their knowledge of how things work.

 English Language Learners

Young writers need the opportunity to use the language for authentic communication. Directions are authentic. Directions have to make readers or listeners do what the writer or speaker directs.

Begin by promoting oral work in the native language. Pair together children who speak the same language, put a divider between them at eye-level, and direct one to give directions to the other for drawing a square. Direct the other to give directions for drawing a triangle. They should compare their drawings and give each other feedback for how their directions could be made more clear. They can write the directions in their native language or in English, but the key here is clarity. Clarity is not language specific; it works in any language.

Perform the same operation in the second language (English). Compare the extent to which they were able to communicate the task clearly in both the native language and English. Then see if the communication is more or less clear when the children get to select the task themselves.

Writing Directions

1. Write a direction sentence for making the first line in a rectangle.

   _____

   _____

2. Write a direction sentence for making the second line in a rectangle.

   _____

   _____

3. Write a direction sentence for making the third line in a rectangle.

   _____

   _____

4. Write a direction sentence for making the fourth line in a rectangle.

   _____

   _____

92   Get Writing!! Book 2 Grades 2-3   ©ECS Learning Systems, Inc., San Antonio, TX

5. Write your four sentences on a separate piece of paper, being careful not to use the word rectangle anywhere. Ask a partner to read and follow your directions. Don't explain anything or help at all. And don't argue. Just let your partner follow your directions.

After your partner has followed your directions, ask him or her to explain to you how your directions were easy or hard to follow. Ask how your directions could be changed to make them better. Then return to your desk and rewrite your directions so they will be better.

_____

_____

_____

_____

_____

6. Now, give your new directions to another partner and see how well they work. You may rewrite your directions one more time.

11 Writing About How Things Are Alike and Different

—The sentence, as a whole piece of writing, can accommodate any attempt to write about likenesses and differences.

 ## Information for the Teacher

Learning to compare and contrast in writing does not necessarily require long pieces of writing, but it does require whole pieces of writing. Of course, in later years longer essays will be assigned. This activity is designed to prepare second- and third-graders for such writing, to give them several years of thinking about how to compare and contrast in writing.

Writing About How Things Are Alike and Different allows young writers to enter the compare/contrast mode of discourse at the sentence level. Much of this activity should be oral. Young writers should talk about how things are alike and different. They should write sentences on paper, but they should have likenesses and differences firmly organized in their minds first.

The use of figurative language in this lesson is natural, even for very young children. Even though we suggest you do not emphasize matters of simile and metaphor, you will notice that these constructions occur naturally in children's ideas. Call attention to these constructions if you like, but it is best for second- and third-graders to think about writing sentences about likenesses and differences, rather than working to be figurative and remembering the literary terms. There is plenty of time for that.

Finally, as with every other lesson in this book, it is important that young writers think about how they can use what they are learning in their everyday writing. Therefore, once the idea of a sentence comparing two things appears to be clear to most of the children, encourage them to use such sentences in a real context as quickly as possible.

 ## Objective

Young writers will think in and compose sentences that show how two or more things are alike and how two or more things are different. Eventually, they will write at least two sentences that both compare and contrast.

©ECS Learning Systems, Inc., San Antonio, TX

 ## Conducting the Lesson

1. **Introduce the idea of describing something by telling what it is like or not like.** Choose something the children are familiar with. When someone thinks they know what the object is, have him/her whisper their guess to you.

   Example: "I have something in this box. I want to give you a clue. It's like a very small bowl with a long handle. You all know what this object is, but to write about it for someone who has never seen one, I would want to describe it in a way that the person could understand. What do you think I might be writing about?" (A pan?) "The handle looks like a stick that has been smashed flat, except that it's metal, not wood, and the color of a dime or a quarter." (I know! I know!) "Come whisper to me." (A spoon?)

2. **Ask the student to tell the class, without giving it away, which clue helped him/her guess correctly.**

   Example: "Without telling what is in the box, tell the class what I said that helped you know what is in there." (When you said the handle is like a dime or quarter.) "How about the part where I said it looks like a small dish with a long handle?" (It was the color.) "Do you know what color dimes and quarters are?" (Yeah, they're silver.)

3. **Ask the student to give the class a new clue that might help them figure out what the object is.** When they all know what the object is, point out, through discussion, how the combination of clues helped them figure it out.

   Example: "Now you think of a clue that will compare what's in the box with something we all know about, and see if your clue will help everyone else." (It's like a fork and knife.) [Hands go up.] "That was a good one, I think. Now, do you all know what it is? Okay, if you think it's a silver dollar, raise your hand. Okay, how about a spoon? If you think it's a spoon, raise your hand." [Hands shoot up.]

Cue

Write a sentence that shows how two things are alike. Write a sentence that shows how two things are different. Write one or more sentences that shows how two things are alike and different.

Get Writing!! Book 2 Grades 2-3   ©ECS Learning Systems, Inc., San Antonio, TX   95

"How did you know?" (Jeff said it is like a knife and fork.) "How did this clue help you?" (I just knew because of the color and the handle thing you said.) "Oh, so it wasn't just one comparison, one clue. It was all the comparisons, all the ways it is like other things." (Yeah, all the clues said it was a spoon.)

4. **Engage the students in a discussion about how to write sentences that show how one thing is like another.**

   Example: "Think of a toy you especially like. I want you to think of a way to tell about the toy by comparing it with something else." (It's like a soldier.) "Oh, that must be a good comparison because everyone knows." (It's GI Joe.) "If I had never seen GI Joe, how could you describe the toy so I would be able to picture what it looks like?" (Maybe I could say that GI Joe is an army man dressed in colors like trees and plants in a forest.) "Who can picture this GI Joe?" [Hands go up, and students offer the colors of GI Joe's camouflage clothing.]

5. **Come back to the activity on the following day, and regularly, until the students are able to write well-constructed descriptive sentences.** Urge them to use their comparison sentences in the stories they are writing, or their reports, poems, or letter to Grandma thanking her for the scarf she sent as a birthday present.

6. **When most of the children seem to understand comparison sentences, move to sentences that tell about differences between two things.** Provide examples, and lead them through oral and written sentences according to the procedures above. (For example, differences between people they know, between two places they go, between two rooms in their house, and so forth).

Tip

Remember, it isn't just practice that makes perfect; it's perfect practice that makes perfect.

 ## Daily Writing Activities

1. Write a comparison sentence that shows the color of a sunset.

2. Write a comparison sentence that shows how it feels to be thirsty.

3. Write a comparison sentence that makes a picture of mud.

4. Write a comparison sentence that shows an angry lion.

5. Write a comparison sentence that shows what ice cream feels like when you eat it.

6. Write a comparison sentence that shows what happens when you eat ice cream too fast.

7. Write a comparison sentence that will help readers know how big your bedroom is at home.

8. Write a comparison sentence that shows how you felt on the hottest day of the year.

9. Write a sentence to show how one of your toys is different from another of your toys. (**Note to Teacher:** In this activity it might be helpful to show children how they can put two pieces, or clauses, of a sentence together and join them with a coordinating conjunction. It isn't necessary, or even useful for that matter, to teach the terminology associated with a compound sentence. Most people can write a sentence with two independent clauses separated with a coordinating conjunction, without ever hearing these terms. However, in writing about a contrast, it is helpful to have a sample sentence available. An example might be: **My Legos blocks are my favorite toys to play with, but my Barbie doll is prettier.** That sort of construction is useful in a contrast sentence.)

 It is important to understand that most, but not all, in the room will understand and be able to use these kinds of sentences in their everyday writing. There is time. The purpose of **Writing About How Things Are Alike and Different** is to introduce and practice the ideas. Some young writers will need even more introductory material, but this is a start.

Get Writing!! Book 2 Grades 2-3   ©ECS Learning Systems, Inc., San Antonio, TX   97

10. Write a sentence that shows how two of your favorite television programs are different.

11. Write a sentence that shows how two books you have read are different.

12. Write a sentence that shows how rain and snow are different.

13. Write a sentence in which you show how two of your friends are different from each other.

14. Write a sentence that tells how the characters in two books you have read recently are different from each other.

15. Write a sentence in which you show how your state is different from another state about the same size.

16. Write a double sentence string to show how you are like one of your friends and different, as well.

17. Write a double sentence string about two birthday parties you've had. Show how they were similar and how they were different.

18. Write a piece about three kinds of snack food. Show how they are alike and how they are different.

©ECS Learning Systems, Inc., San Antonio, TX

 ## Across the Curriculum

Several of the daily activities in this section suggest applications across the curriculum. For instance, using Activity 15, an excellent writing activity can come from showing the difference between Alabama and Pennsylvania.

Example: Pennsylvania and Alabama are similar as steel makers and coal users, but they're different because they're in different regions of the country. They're similar because they are both heavily wooded, but they're different because Pennsylvania is more heavily populated.

Second- and third-graders can do the same kinds of writings about Arizona and New Mexico, Kansas and Nebraska, Texas and Alaska, and Connecticut and Massachusetts.

For a mathematical application, consider how addition and multiplication or division and subtraction are alike and different. Too complex for second- and third-graders? Perhaps for some, but not for all.

How is an island different from a peninsula? How are they alike? How are population maps similar to and different from each other? How are police officers and mail carriers alike and different?

 ## English Language Learners

Because so much of what compare and contrast language is about comes from the experiences and perceptions of the language user, this is an excellent activity for youngsters whose native language is not English. There is a good bit of experience in the backgrounds of children who speak a native language other than English (especially those who are recent immigrants). These experiences can be part of the oral and written activity, whether in English or the native language.

For example, there are modes of dress, traditions, and places around the world to compare. There are a wide variety of dishes to compare, such as the way rice is prepared in various parts of East Asia, the Middle East, and the Americas. It seems nearly everyone eats a grain-based staple like bread; the fried bread of the Navajo, the piki bread of the Hopi, and the enriched flour bread of suburban Cleveland are similar in function and even in basic preparation, yet vastly different in taste, texture, and nutritional value. Children might talk about, write about, and share the rich variety of foods and recipes they bring with them from their parts of the world.

©ECS Learning Systems, Inc., San Antonio, TX

Language Activity Sheet
Writing About How Things
Are Alike and Different

Nearly everyone in the world includes something made from grain in their diets. In the United States, it's bread. In Mexico it's tortillas. Among indigenous peoples in the United States, the bread is very different from tribe to tribe.

1. What is the name of the grain-based food you and your parents eat during your mealtimes?

   _____

2. What is the grain in that grain-based food you and your parents eat at mealtime?

   _____

3. What else might be used to make that grain-based food you and your parents eat at mealtime?

   _____

4. Now, exchange your paper with someone else and compare the name, the grain, and the rest of the ingredients. Talk with your partner about how the food you and your parents eat is similar to and different from the food eaten by your partner and his or her parents.

5. Write a sentence that tells how the foods are similar.

   _____

   _____

©ECS Learning Systems, Inc., San Antonio, TX

6. Write a sentence that tells how the foods are different.

_____

_____

7. Write a sentence about how your grain-based food tastes.

_____

_____

8. After talking to your partner, write a sentence about how his or her grain-based food tastes.

_____

_____

9. Write a sentence that shows how the taste of the two kinds of grain-based food is either alike or different.

_____

_____

12 Word Limiters: Writing Short

—We can tell youngsters about writing with clarity and precision, but doing it has power far beyond the telling.

Information for the Teacher

Young writers need to learn that writing is a precise skill reflective of clear thinking and careful arrangements of words and ideas. Writing this way requires young people to know what they are writing about and how to use just the right words to get it done.

Word Limiters demands perseverance and attention. This isn't what young writers do ordinarily. It isn't a natural kind of writing, and even adults who write for a living don't write this way very often. However, it is a useful activity for young writers because it is so demanding.

It is important to understand that this activity, and most others for that matter, won't connect with all young writers well or at the same time. It will be too hard for some for a while, and for a few, all year. It will seem boring to some early on, for some all the time. Several, perhaps even many, will pursue the challenge diligently and as a result become clearer thinkers and more disciplined writers (at second- and third-grade levels, of course).

On another level, there is no suggestion in this activity that children should write as little as possible just so they can be done with it. The reality here is that writing short pieces can be harder than writing long pieces, and it often takes more time. It takes more skill to write short rather than long, and writing skill is what these lessons are about.

Objective

Young writers will write descriptions and explanations under word-length limitations. The writing will occur as initial best-effort drafts, progressively shortening the description until it cannot be further shortened without compromising the ideas or images.

It is very important that we understand and convey to young writers that writing short does *not* mean writing less. As will become quite apparent in this lesson, writing short, at least in **Word Limiters**, often means writing *more*.

 ## Conducting the Lesson

1. **Give students a cue for writing a sentence.** Write a well-constructed student sentence on the board, then ask the class to suggest words that will make the sentence more descriptive. Write this new sentence on the board and ask the students to count the words.

   Example: "Let's begin with one of those sentences we have been writing before morning recess every day. Think of a sentence that contains the ideas **old man**, **vehicle**, **weather**." (**An old man was driving his car in the rain.**) "That's a good one. Now, everyone, we need to be able to see that man, that rain, that car, and you have to do this in only one sentence. See what you can do." (**The wrinkled grandfather drove his pickup truck with a camper shell in the rain and hail storm.**) "There are 17 words in this sentence. It's a fine sentence and has all the assigned ideas in it, and it paints a pretty good picture, too."

2. **Introduce the idea of removing one, then two, then three words from the sentence.** Remind the students to choose words that will not change the picture the sentence makes.

   Example: "This sentence has 17 words in it. Can you think of a way to take out one word without changing the word picture?" (Take out **shell** because if you have a truck with a camper, you know it is a camper without **shell**.) "So read the sentence without that one word." (**The wrinkled grandfather drove his pickup truck with a camper in the rain and hail storm.**)

   "The picture is still the same?" (Yeah.) "Let's see if we can hold onto the picture and take out one more word so the sentence will have 15 words." (Take out *truck* because when you say pickup, it's the same as *truck*.) "So write the sentence." (**The wrinkled grandfather drove his pickup with a camper in the rain and hail storm.**)

   "Can you take out another word and not ruin the word picture? If you have an idea, read your new sentence. Remember, this time the sentence will have only 14 words." (**The wrinkled grandfather drove his pickup with a camper in the cold wet storm.**) "I'll bet you can rewrite it in 13 words." (**The wrinkled grandfather drove his camper in the cold wet storm.**) "That one is in 11 words. You cut two words that time, and all the ideas are still there. That's terrific! I want you to notice how you were able to change the writing to make the sentence shorter without changing the ideas. That's what we are going to do for the next week or two. We are going to try to write big ideas in small numbers of words."

Cue   In 10 to 15 words, tell about what a rose looks like.

Word Limiters: Writing Short

3. **At the beginning of writing period the following day, remind the students about the previous day's Writing Short activity.** Then write the following piece on the board and ask a student to read it and count the words.

   Example: Garfield the cat was sleeping on a soft and fluffy rug. He was dreaming of a fat piece of chocolate cake. He woke up and looked all around for the cake he was eating in his dream. He couldn't find it anywhere.

4. **Ask the students to select a word to remove that will not change the meaning or picture of the sentence.**

   Example: "When you find a word to take out, write it on your paper. If you have a word to spell, and you don't know how to spell it, remember the rule: *Write it so you can read it as long as your paper is on your side of the desk. When it crosses the desk, it has to be right.*"

5. **Ask the students to select a second word to remove.**

   Example: "Now I want you to write another word you can take out. Remember, sometimes we can take out a word if we rewrite a sentence, or when we put sentences together. But we can't change the meaning just to take out a word. When you find another word to take out, write it on your paper."

6. **Conduct a conversation about which words they took out and the effect of the removal on meaning, clarity, and so forth.** The teacher must be the judge here. Can we, for example, remove *soft* if *fluffy* remains? If we're writing short, and have two words that mean close to the same thing, only the better of the two remain. That doesn't mean two words that mean nearly the same thing should never be used in a sentence or paragraph. It means when we're writing short, trying to be as precise and as brief as possible, one right word is better than two near-right words.

7. **Over time, lead the children into drafting short, instead of merely revising to shorten.** Both are important. Revising to shorten aids young writers in understanding revision as something other than adding punctuation and making it more legible.

   Drafting short, however, helps introduce them to care when drafting. Young writers need to learn what practicing writers know. That is, always write as well as possible, even in the draft. Some children believe writing well is not important when writing the draft. Writers know, of course, that this is not the case, and it is never too early to help youngsters understand it.

 Daily Writing Activities

1. In one sentence, tell what a police officer does.

2. In one sentence of no more than 10 words, tell two things about George Washington.

3. Write one sentence of no more than 10 words that tells what **cute** means.

4. In only one sentence, tell what a toaster does in the kitchen.

5. Use only one sentence to tell what your favorite candy bar is and why.

6. Think of as many things as you can that tell about what a butterfly looks like. Write one sentence that tells as many things as possible about what a butterfly looks like.

7. Look at the sentence you wrote for number six and rewrite it so it has three fewer words.

8. Write a sentence of not more than 10 words that tells what your best friend looks like.

9. In no fewer than 10 words, and no more than 15, describe the difference between **grapefruit** and **lemon**.

10. Describe the main character in your favorite storybook. You may use two sentences, but you may not write more than 16 words.

11. Find North Carolina on a map of the United States. In one sentence, use the names of three states to describe where North Carolina is located.

12. Find out what a violet is. Write a description of a violet in no more than 11 words.

13. Write a report about the state (or other country) where you were born. You have to put in as much information as you can, but you may not write more than 30 words.

14. What is a tostado? Write about a tostado in two sentences and not more than 13 words.

 Never wait for the last child to be finished during writing period. If we wait for the last one, most of the children are bored with the wait time. Remember, the teacher controls the time in the class.

15. Retell the story of Cinderella, using no more than 20 words.

16. Write the name of your favorite sports team. Now, explain why it is your favorite team, but don't write more than 12 words.

17. Tell all about the last field trip you took with your class. Then change what you wrote so there are six fewer words.

18. Tell all about your favorite television program in no fewer than 15 words and no more than 25 words.

19. Write a piece about your favorite food for dinner. Write it in less than 15 words and no more than 20 words.

20. Think about a refrigerator. Write about it so someone who has never seen one will know what it is. You may not write more than 20 words.

 Across the Curriculum

Word Limiters can be applied to any sort of writing for any purpose. Science, however, is an especially appropriate application because one of its main purposes is to learn to observe carefully and report on the observation. In school, young writers need to observe scientific happenings and write precisely about them. This precision can be promoted with **Word Limiters**.

For example, children can plant lima beans in paper cups, place some of the cups on the window sill and some in a closet, observe germination over several days, then describe what they did and the result. When the conversation is complete and drafts of the reports are finished, announce that all reports have to be changed by removing eight words without changing the meanings and information. On another occasion, observation reports might be written in less than 20 and no more than 25 words.

 English Language Learners

Young people who speak a native language other than English usually learn conversational English relatively quickly, so they can play effectively with the English-speaking children. **Word Limiters** helps bridge the gap between social and classroom language performance.

Evidence in cognitive psychology attests to the critical relationship between concentration and learning. A difference between social language and classroom language is the degree of consciousness necessary for classroom language. Classroom language is far more formal, more purposeful, more deliberate. The demands of **Word Limiters** are formal language demands. When young writers are told to eliminate a certain number of words from a piece already carefully written, they are forced to consider each word, each idea.

Language Activity Sheet

Word Limiters: Writing Short

A lonely hawk floated on the warm air and watched the ground below for prey.

1. The sentence above has 15 words in it. In the space below, write what you think is the main idea of the sentence.

____

____

2. Rewrite the sentence about the hawk in 14 words.

____

____

3. Now rewrite it again, this time in 12 words.

____

____

4. Read the sentence you just wrote, and make sure the main idea is the same as what you wrote in Number 1. Write the main idea of your sentence in Number 2 in the space below.

____

____

5. Paying very careful attention to your main idea in Number 4, rewrite the sentence in only eight words.

_____

_____

6. The sentence at the top of this activity sheet has at least six different ideas in it. Put a check beside each of the ideas in the sentence you wrote for Number 5.

_____ hawk   _____ where it was looking

_____ how it flew   _____ what it was looking for

_____ where it was flying

_____ what it did

7. If all six ideas are not in your sentence under Number 5, write the sentence again and try to get all of the ideas in it.

_____

_____

_____

13 People Talk to Each Other: Writing Dialogue

—The way dialogue is written can separate good stories from all the rest.

 ## Information for the Teacher

Writers reveal much about their characters by the way they make them talk. We do not expect all second- and third-graders to write scintillating dialogue. However, young writers can learn very quickly to make their characters talk and their stories better.

The focus in **People Talk To Each Other** is the authenticity of characters' speech. Young writers must pay attention to their characters to do what Faulkner said he did: *Invent a character and follow him around for a few days.* Faulkner's notion was to let the character do the talking and write it down as it comes out. Young writers need to know their characters, to listen to them, to hear them talk, and cause them to talk in ways that fit who they are. That is what this activity is about.

There is also a mechanical matter associated with writing dialogue. In this section, young writers will learn to use quotation marks and line punctuation (periods, question marks, and commas) when quotation marks occur. Because context is everything in writing, the **People Talk To Each Other** activity includes both the dialogue and mechanics activities necessary to make dialogue work. Also emphasized is how to avoid the repeated use of *he said* and *she said* to denote speakers.

 ## Objective

Young writers will make their characters talk. They will show the talk in written form, and the dialogue will be clear, partly because it is mechanically accurate.

Tip

This lesson is complex; each part can consume a lot of time. However, it only works when needed, and in the context of the children's own stories. We have the responsibility to teach students how to use dialogue properly. Because of its complexity, this kind of writing is usually reinforced at high school and university levels.

 ## Conducting the Lesson

1. **Introduce a two-character interaction.** Solicit suggestions for dialogue from volunteers. Write the first line of the dialogue on the board.

   Example: "Class, let's pretend we have a girl about your age. She is working in the painting center at an easel. At the next easel is a boy who has a jar of yellow paint. She wants to borrow the yellow paint. What do you think will happen here?" (She will ask him for it.) "What will she say?" (**Can I borrow your yellow paint?**) "So she will ask a question." (Yes.)

2. **Write the character's first line on the board and read it aloud.** Ask the students to identify the speaker. Explain that the writer must tell the reader who is speaking.

   Example: [**May I borrow your yellow paint?**] "Now let's pretend the picture we are looking at is in writing. Readers have to know who is talking. The girl is going to say, '**May I borrow your yellow paint?**' How will we tell our readers what the girl said?" (Just write it down. Write the question.) "If I write, '**May I borrow your yellow paint?**' who am I asking? This question just says somebody is asking somebody for yellow paint. How do we tell the reader who is talking and who is being talked to?"

3. **As students make suggestions, introduce the proper way to punctuate a question in dialogue.**

   Example: "In '**May I borrow your yellow paint?**' the girl is asking a question, and the question mark is part of what she said. We use quotation marks to show what our characters have said. The quotation mark at the end goes outside of the question mark."

4. **On the board, put the quotation mark outside of the question mark.** Then, ask the students to identify the character who is asking the question.

   Example: "Now, we know someone in the story said this. But who?" (The girl. After what she said. Make it say, "**May I borrow your yellow paint? she asked.**" Write *she asked* after the question.)

Cue

Think about how two people would talk with one another. Write a short scene in which they share a thought.

"How do I put an end to the sentence?" (It's already finished.) "But, there has to be something to show the sentence is finished." (Put a period, then.) "Where?" (After *she said*.) [Point to a spot after *said*.] "Here?" (Yes.) [Place a period after *she said*.]

5. **Continue with the interaction, writing student suggestions for dialogue on the board and commenting on word choice and punctuation.**

   Example: "What do you think will happen next?" (He will stop painting and look at her. Then he will say it's okay, and he will give her the paint.) "How are we going to write that down?" (Put that he says okay and gives her the paint.) "Like this?: **He says okay and gives her the paint.**"

   (It could be like that, but I think it should be that he said okay and handed her the paint.) "Exactly, what do you think we should write next?" (That it's okay.) "You want me to write, up here, the words *that it's okay*?" (No, just say '**It's okay. You can use the yellow, he said.**') "Well now, that will work."

   "Is that what you mean?" (Yes, but you have to put quotations in.) "Okay, let's do some thinking about that. Where do they go, in front of the comma or after it?" (After the comma.)

6. **On a following day, develop another two-character, two-line interaction.** This second activity will go much faster than the first.

7. **After completing several two-character, two-line interactions,** introduce alternatives to noting the characters' dialogue with *he said* or *she said*.

Example: "Class, you are writing interactions between two characters very well. Let's look at something a little different. Pretend we have that girl and boy again, and the girl asks for the paint. Let's look at what we have so far:

> **'May I borrow the yellow paint?' she asked**

> **'It's okay. You can use the yellow,' he said.**

"I think he would turn to her before he talked. I might write it like this: **He turned to her. 'It's okay. You can use the yellow.'"**

"Who is talking here?" (The boy) "How do you know?" (Because we just know.) "Look what I did here. When I wrote that he turned toward the girl, you thought about the boy. This is one way we can show what our characters say without always writing *he said* or *she said*."

As students use dialogue in everyday writing, resist the temptation to make mechanical corrections. Individual conferences take enormous time, so spend just long enough to remind students of the lessons, and encourage him/her to try to make the mechanical editions. In a longer conference, a more detailed discussion can be had in the context of the child's authentic writing.

As the instructional sets move along, call attention to how dialogue is handled in literature readings. Occasionally, throughout the year, call attention to how the speaker is identified without using *he said* or *she said*. Encourage students to attempt the less direct identification by saying something about the speaker to identify him/her or by indenting.

People Talk To Each Other: Writing Dialogue

Daily Writing Activities

1. Write a two-character, two-line dialogue between a boy and a girl getting ready to start a baseball game.

2. Write a two-character, two-line dialogue between you and your mother about whether you may have a second piece of cake after dinner.

3. Write a two-character, two-line dialogue between your father or mother and one of his/her friends about having a picnic. You may use *he said* or *she said* no more than one time.

4. Write a two-character, two-line dialogue between you and someone in your class about borrowing a pencil.

5. Write a two-character, three-line dialogue between you and a friend in your class just before going out to recess.

6. Write a two-character, three-line dialogue between a turkey and a man just before Thanksgiving. You may use *he said* or *she said* no more than one time.

7. Write a two-character, three-line dialogue between Jack and the Giant.

8. Write a two-character, four-line dialogue between two animals in the forest just as they smell smoke from a forest fire.

9. Write a two-character, four-line dialogue between someone who plays a violin in an orchestra and the conductor of the orchestra.

10. Write a two-character, four-line dialogue between the President of the United States and one of his secret service agents.

Tip

As these activities are presented, point out the following mechanical rules for writing dialogue:

- Quotation marks go outside all line punctuation (with the exception of colons, semicolons, and question marks, when the words in quotations aren't a question). However, since most of their writing is usually less complex than this, it is not necessary to burden second- and third-graders with these exceptions.

- Every time the speaker changes, the writer begins a new line and indents, just like starting a new paragraph.

11. Write a two-character, five-line dialogue that takes place on a bridge high above a river. One of the characters is a child who is very scared.

12. Write the dialogue between Snow White and her stepmother when the stepmother tells her that she will have to leave the castle. You may use *he said* or *she said* only two times.

13. Pretend that a large rock on a mountainside could talk. Write the dialogue between the rock and a tree that is growing nearby.

14. Write a dialogue between two characters in your favorite television program.

15. Write a two-character dialogue between two children who are yelling at each other on the playground because they do not agree about whether a base runner was safe or out.

16. Write a dialogue between you and one of your friends as you leave a movie that you both thought was terrific. You may use *he said* or *she said* only once.

17. Write a dialogue between two people in a television commercial about a breakfast cereal.

18. Write a dialogue between two police officers having lunch.

19. Write a dialogue between you and one of your friends as you talk on the telephone.

20. Write a dialogue between two people who have just seen a boy fall while riding his bicycle. The boy who fell is not hurt badly, but he is crying.

Get Writing!!

Get Writing!! Book 2 Grades 2-3   ©ECS Learning Systems, Inc., San Antonio, TX   115

 Across the Curriculum

For second- and third-graders, dialogue writing usually occurs in the context of story writing. Since story writing occurs mainly during language arts time, it would appear that applications across the curriculum would be a stretch. However, dialogue can occur as oral and written language to help clarify students' understanding of different content areas.

- Direct second- and third-graders to write about the question-answer session between the President of the United States and their minister, their grandmother, the mayor, or even themselves.

- What would the talk sound like if the biographical focus they are studying in February were to include sitting and talking with George Washington or Abraham Lincoln or the current President of the United States?

- In a science unit on protecting the environment, what would the dialogue be between someone committed to protecting forests and someone whose parent works in the timber industry and makes a living from cutting trees? In a science unit exploring the water cycle, youngsters might write dialogues between a lake and the sun.

116   Get Writing!! Book 2 Grades 2-3   ©ECS Learning Systems, Inc., San Antonio, TX

 ## English Language Learners

Dialogue writing is a perfect opportunity to write in the everyday language of social interaction. While much of the writing in school is at the level of cognitive academic language, dialogue is more basic communication. Each idea in this lesson provides opportunities for children whose native language is not English to apply authentic language to the classroom.

People Talk To Each Other: Writing Dialogue

Pretend that you are sitting on a park bench waiting for your mother or father to come and take you home. An elderly woman sits beside you. She is dressed in a heavy overcoat even though it is a summer day, and she is carrying two plastic grocery bags. She stays at the end of the bench, alone. She is the first one to talk.

1. Write what you think she says to you.

_____

_____

_____

_____

2. You have been taught not to talk with strangers, but you have to stay on this bench. You can't just not pay any attention to the woman. Write what you say in answer or response to what she said.

_____

_____

_____

©ECS Learning Systems, Inc., San Antonio, TX

3. She wants to keep talking. Her voice is soft and warm. She stays at the far end of the bench. After what you said to her, what do you think she says?

_____

_____

_____

4. Now your mother or father comes up to the bench. What do you think your mother or father will say to the old woman?

_____

_____

_____

5. As you walk away, what do you think you will say to your mother or father?

_____

_____

_____

14 Writing the News

—Much insight can come from writing the kinds of language that occur in newspapers.

Information for the Teacher

Being in touch with the news is important for citizens in a free society. Thomas Jefferson seemed to honor the connection between the citizen and the newspaper when he wrote, "Were it left to me to decide whether we should have a government without newspapers or newspapers without government, I should not hesitate to prefer the latter." There are many different newspapers, and it is a laudable goal of schooling to teach young people how to read and use them.

Writing the News begins an experience that will last the whole time students are in school and their whole lives thereafter. This might be the most important writing any of us ever do; not so much because of the writing, but for the reading that comes from the writing connection. As they write the news, young writers become increasingly able to understand how the newspapers operate and how news is selected and written. They become better news readers.

This activity will emphasize two kinds of newspaper writing. Straight news is about writing clearly and accurately what you see (or otherwise sense). Opinion writing is about organizing and presenting one's opinion about something, often from the straight news. (The former receives far more attention in the second and third grades.)

Objective

Young writers will report on what they purposefully observe. Later they will report on something that happens without warning. Their reports will be both oral and written. They will also form and report their opinions regarding items in their local news. They will be encouraged to formulate these opinions to include reasons and conclusions.

Conducting the Lesson

1. **Prepare a scenario with two sixth-graders, a boy and a girl, to simulate a "news story in the making."**

    Example: At a specific time unknown to the class, two sixth-graders enter your room, walk to the pencil sharpener and sharpen a pencil, then gather several books, a tablet, something from the teacher's desk, and something small from a bulletin board. On their way out of the room, one says something nonsensical to the other like, "Boogaloo." They don't talk to one another, to the teacher, or to any of the students while they are in the room. In fact, they don't even look at anyone while they are in the room. Without running, they move as quickly as possible. There is no warning of their pending arrival, and when they leave they do not return.

2. **Ask students to tell what they saw happen.** There will be some laughter in the room, but mostly the students won't know what to make of what just happened. That's the best circumstance under which to conduct the following conversation. Listen to their versions of what happened, reinforce their observations and memories, and eventually ask some questions.

    Example:
    a. How many people came into the room?
    b. Who was taller, the boy or the girl?
    c. What color socks was the girl wearing?
    d. What did the boy carry out of the room?
    e. What did the girl carry out of the room?
    f. Who took the pin from the bulletin board?
    g. What was the name of the book the boy took from the shelf?
    h. What color was the boy's hair?
    i. How many things did they carry away?
    j. What did they take from my desk?
    k. What time was it when they came in?
    l. How long were they here?
    m. Which one talked on the way out the door?
    n. What did (s)he say on the way out the door?

Cue

Observe something and write what you have observed. Take a position on something, and write a piece about your opinion.

Writing the News

There are endless possibilities for questions. It is likely that several students will notice and remember a fair amount of what went on. It is just as likely that many students will be bowled over by the event and will have noticed and remembered very few details.

3. **Ask those who seem to remember a fair amount of what happened to orally report on the event as well as they can.** Tell them to use as many details as possible in their oral reports. Encourage statements like, "This is what happened… This is what I saw… This is who they were…" Discourage statements like, "I think there were …. Maybe they …." When the conversation is finished, direct the students to take the next eight to ten minutes to write about the incident.

Have a newspaper article or maybe a copy of *Weekly Reader* handy, and show how the news articles are authoritative and factual. In sections of the newspaper, the writing is not about what people *think* about what happened, it is about what *happened*. This activity is about observing and writing the news.

Tip

This isn't a trap to show the students they aren't observant or don't remember well. It is an object lesson about observing and reporting.

4. **Follow this lesson over several days with more conversation about news writing.** Read excerpts of news articles to the class and share the construction of the newspaper with them.

Direct the students to make observations on their way home after school over the course of several days. Suggest they count the number of trash cans, the trees on the south side of each street, the colors of flowers, the German or American cars, etc.

Tip

Check to see if the local newspaper has a classroom newspaper program. If it does not, take a field trip to the local newspaper office, or bring a reporter from the newspaper at a local high school or university to the classroom to talk about news writing.

©ECS Learning Systems, Inc., San Antonio, TX

Writing the News

5. **Three or four days after the first "news in the making" incident, schedule another "visit," this time by different students who do different things.** The class will be far more observant this time. They will know they are in an object lesson, and will suddenly watch everything. When the visitors leave, direct the class to make a list of everything they think happened—without talking to each other about it.

   Don't give them as much time as they think they need. Listen to several lists and call attention to their ability to observe and remember by saying something like, "Paying attention is something we will be practicing all year."

   Everyone should write the incident as a news report, noting sequence and details. This activity assumes that most student sentences will tell most of what actually happened. For second- and third-graders, that is sufficient.

6. **Later in the second-grade year or sometime during the third-grade year, set the framework for writing an editorial piece.** Choose something reasonably controversial that affects each student personally. After making the announcement, pause through the uproar, and when the class settles down, ask them what they think. On the board, write a sentence that represents their responses. Explain that they must have good reasons to support their opinions, and make a separate list of their reasons on the board. Finally, help them determine the two most important reasons and to summarize by restating their opinion.

   Example: "Class, I have some news for you. The principal and teachers have noticed too much noise during the lunch period, so we will have our lunch at 10:00 in the morning instead of at noon, and we will have to eat in our classroom without going outside. What do you think about this decision?" (Not fair!) (Not right!) (Not hungry at 10:00!) (What about play time at lunch?) (What about lunch buyers?) "How many of you think it isn't fair?" [On the board, write: **The students in the second grade think the new lunch program of eating in their classroom at 10:00 a.m. is unfair.**]

   "Does this pretty much say what you think?" (Yes. It isn't fair.) "Why isn't it fair? You have to have reasons that everyone can understand." (I'm not hungry then.) (We can't play with the other kids.) (I have to eat at noon because of my medicine.) (My mom gets home at noon to make my lunch, and I'm a walker.) "What's the most important reason why the lunch program isn't fair? Which one, for example, affects the most of us?" (The play one.) "All right, we have to say that in our essay about what we think." [Write the second sentence in the essay: **We think it is unfair because we won't get to play with the other kids after lunch.**]

©ECS Learning Systems, Inc., San Antonio, TX

"Is that correct?" (Yeah.) "What's the next most important reason?" (We'll be really hungry in the afternoon if we eat that early.) [Write that reason in a sentence on the board.] "Now, class, we have to finish our opinion essay. You said the program is unfair, and you gave two reasons why. Now we have to write a sentence that summarizes what we have written so far. We need to write a last sentence that reminds readers of what we have written already. What do you think?" (It's not fair to take our play time away and we won't be hungry anyway.) [Write this sentence on the board: **We think the new lunch policy is unfair because we don't have our play time and it is too early in the day.**]

"Does that say what you had in mind?" (Yes. Is it really true about the lunch?) "Well, if it were true, you would have something to send to the principal and all the teachers that tells what you think."

7. **Debrief.** As the year rolls along, bring other instances of possible controversy to the students and encourage them to think systematically to express their sentiments in writing. The system is to write about the following:

   a. The issue

   b. Their position on the issue

   c. The reasons

   d. Summarizing statement that pulls it all together

Once students accomplish this several times under your leadership, refer them to the editorial page(s) of the newspaper. Show them how editorial writers include all four parts in their writing, and that every one of their editorials is about an opinion.

Tip

This lesson is more about awareness than performance. Students age seven and eight certainly have opinions. But the matter of seeing issues from more than one perspective, which is fundamental to a reasoned and well-crafted editorial, is developmentally a year or more away. Nevertheless, if they are introduced to and participate in such thinking, they will have the prior knowledge necessary for a serious start in the next year or two.

 Daily Writing Activities

1. Develop a classroom newspaper in which groups of students have responsibilities for sections or events. One group writes about recess, another about what the class is working on in each subject area. One will write about school-wide matters, and so forth. The whole paper might only be a page or two long, but divided into groups, everyone would have an opportunity to do some news writing. In an editorial section, essays must present issues according to the four points in the system (see page 124, Number 7).

2. Make a major issue out of the *Weekly Reader*. Students should read and study it, noticing how the pieces are written with attention to style, clarity, and objectivity.

3. Use the local newspaper as a resource. Display various articles daily on a newspaper bulletin board. Call attention to how different sections of the newspaper are formatted and to their contents.

4. As they become increasingly aware of the newspaper, students will also become increasingly aware of the news itself. They should then report on current events orally each day, or at least several times each week. They may talk about information from photographs or articles. The class can listen to see if the 5 W's (Who?, What?, Where?, When?, Why?) have been answered. Questions can be asked about what they hear reported.

5. It will be useful to schedule an incident for observation several times each month. It won't take long for the students to become expert at observing, remembering, and reporting.

Get Writing!! Book 2 Grades 2-3   ©ECS Learning Systems, Inc., San Antonio, TX   125

Writing the News

 Across the Curriculum

There is a connection between the news, whether print or electronic, and what happens in the classroom. This connection can become a classroom focus if students are willing to be aware of what they see and hear in the news. Of course, we need to be ready to make adjustments when students bring us material from newspaper and news programs.

Prepare a content-based bulletin board with spaces available for news in mathematics, science, history, geography, art, and so forth. Encourage students to find references for each area of the curriculum. Take one reference each day and read it aloud in class. Direct them to write their own paragraph about the report in the newspaper. Reread the article and set them to work. These paragraphs will be news reports based on news reports.

    ©ECS Learning Systems, Inc., San Antonio, TX

 English Language Learners

The best initial application of **Writing the News** for students whose native language is not English is the classroom newspaper. Its variation accommodates the diversity of students in the classroom. In these two school years (grades two and three), young writers can learn the news styles and mechanical precision so crucial in written communication to a wide audience.

The newspaper could be arranged by sections to include classroom news, school news, and neighborhood news. Sections can also be devoted to the different languages spoken in the classroom and to holidays.

Consider that a classroom with four languages represented also has four cultural backgrounds, four kinds of neighborhoods, four familial constellations, and four holiday patterns represented. The classroom newspaper is a place in which diversity can acquire a printed voice, as students play out who they are and learn from each other.

©ECS Learning Systems, Inc., San Antonio, TX

Language Activity Sheet
Writing the News

1. Make a list of several events in the news right now. Your list may include items from any section of the newspaper or any part of a television or radio news broadcast.

_____ _____

_____ _____

_____ _____

2. With a partner, compare your two lists and what you decide are the most important news items from each of your lists.

_____ _____

_____ _____

_____ _____

3. With your partner, make your list again, but this time put the most important news item first, then the next most important, then the next, and so forth, until you have one news item beside each letter.

(a)   **(d)**

_____   _____

(b)   **(e)**

_____   _____

(c)   **(f)**

_____   _____

©ECS Learning Systems, Inc., San Antonio, TX

4. Write a sentence in the space below that tells how you decided which item would be first, which item would be next, and so forth.

_____

_____

5. You and your partner now join another partnership and compare the two lists of news items. Write their first three news items on the left below and your first three news items on the right below.

_____   _____

_____   _____

_____   _____

6. Write a sentence that tells how you and your partner decided which news item would be first on your list.

_____

_____

15 Writing Informal Letters

—Letter writing is authentic, audience-based writing.

 ## Information for the Teacher

Several attributes of informal letter writing, whether in school or out, are critical to authenticity:

- The letters must be for communication.

- The communication must have an audience.

- The communication must be about something we care about.

- Because the reinforcer for writing a letter is getting an answer, the letters have to be sent on the basis that there is an answer possible.

Writing Informal Letters looks like the traditional second- and third-grade letter assignments we all remember. The teacher graded them and put the ones (s)he liked best on the special bulletin board for special kids and their special work. Most of us wrote informal letters in a writing unit each year, and put our first letters in the mail sometime during our late elementary- or middle-school years.

This informal letter writing lesson is designed to accomplish all four attributes. It has two parts, an intraschool pen pal system and an interschool information exchange. Once the arrangements are made, students can work almost independently, and teachers mostly guide. Additionally, the letter-writing activities described here eliminate the need for postage.

 ## Objective

Second- and third-graders will write at least one informal letter each week for at least two months. The letters will be intraschool informal correspondence with older students and/or interschool correspondence based on information exchange letters with older students.

Tip

An intraschool pen pal and interschool information exchange does not suggest that the more traditional letter-starters cannot or should not be used. In fact, there are several in the daily activities section of this lesson.

Conducting the Lesson

1. **With a fifth- or sixth-grade teacher, arrange an intraschool pen pal exchange with your second- or third-grade students.** Make sure every younger student has an older partner. Explain that on a given day, the letters will be distributed at random to the older students, one to one. Each will read a letter and prepare an appropriate answer.

 *Tip*

> It is important that older students understand that this is an educational experience for the younger students. They have a responsibility to commit the effort that will provide letter writing practice for themselves, as well as an interaction with the younger students.

2. **Lead a conversation focused on informal relationships.** Explain to the students that friendship is built on information, and that by writing back and forth, the writers learn something about each other.

 *Tip*

> If someone says (s)he doesn't want to write to the other person, explain that this is an assignment for the teacher, and all students will write the letter in good faith as well as they can, learn what they can, and be a good partner for the other person.

3. **Explain that the students will write something interesting about themselves in their letters.** Tell them their letters will be delivered to a class of older students who will then answer them in a letter. When they receive these letters, they will each send a letter in reply.

4. **Demonstrate on the board, or the overhead, how to set up an informal letter. Then direct students to write their letters.** They can write the date, the greeting (in this case, "Dear Fifth- (or Sixth-) Grader"), and the closing (or goodbye) in two minutes. The body, or the information, which can be as simple as a sentence or two, might take 10 to 15 minutes to write. It is realistic that most letters will go out with one or more mechanical errors on them. With practice students will learn to eliminate most of these errors.

 Cue

> Write a letter to a friend and tell about something interesting that is happening to you in school.

Writing Informal Letters

5. **When the letters are completed, fold them twice and staple them closed.** Select two mail carriers to carry the letters in a box to the older students' room. The letters should be distributed at random, read seriously, and answered immediately. The older students' letters should be models for the younger writers. They should be clearly written, error-free, and informative.

   The responses should be folded twice, stapled, addressed, and distributed to their young writers on the following day. The younger students' responses will be sent later in the week. If the students write two letters per week, a total of 16 letters will be sent over a two-month period.

   Thus, the intraschool pen pal association is established. This is authentic writing, based on the following:

   - Quantity is important because quantity means practice.

   - Practice is useful because it is associated with a real audience.

   - When the activity is conducted as described, friendships are built, protective associations established, and valuable connections are made between the older and younger students at school.

6. **Extend this activity to an intraschool information exchange with class counterparts at another school in the district, county, even state.** In this activity, students find out what is interesting to others like themselves, and write informal letters back and forth at least once each week for two or three months, or even longer.

Tip

Remind students that as long as the writing is on their side of the desk, its appearance (spelling, punctuation, capitalization, legibility, sentence structure, and so forth) is their own business; but when it crosses the desk, all of that has to be right. They may use the "three-before-me" rule for all revisions:

Students should ask three people for help before asking the teacher. If a child still needs help, write the correct spelling at the top of his/her paper and give a gentle reminder, "Now remember, I don't give spelling words more than once." Put the word on the Word Wall, and direct the children to check it for spelling words.

The first letters are distributed at random. Thereafter, there are partnerships for the exchange. If the two classrooms happen to be online, e-mail partnerships can be established so that the very first letter goes directly to a particular student.

> The distant connections can be established easily enough through teachers at state and national conferences (National Council of Teachers of English, Washington Organization for Reading Development, Texas Joint Council of Teachers of English, etc.). It might be more interesting for your students sharing information with students in another state, but the process will work just fine across town, when necessary.

The key content of the letters is what the students are learning or have learned recently. The exchange is a sharing of information. The letters are short and clear:

> I am learning about how whales migrate from Mexico to Alaska. They have babies called calves in the ocean off Mexico because it's warm there. Then they swim with their calves to the ocean near Alaska for the rest of the year. They know just when they have to go on their trips back and forth.
>
> When you write, tell me what you know about whales, or tell me something about what you are learning.
>
> Yours truly,
> (Name)

The *inter*school information exchange differs from the *intra*school pen pal association in the following ways:

* The information exchange is between two school sites.

* The information exchange is between students in similar grades.

* The information exchange is based on what students are learning or studying.

Writing Informal Letters

 ## Daily Writing Activities

An on-going letter-writing process is embedded in this lesson. The process promotes at least two informal letters every day for at least two months, perhaps even longer. Such a schedule of regular writing activities is authentic and audience-oriented.

However, other kinds of informal letter-writing tasks can be assigned on a regular basis:

1. Write an informal letter to a grandparent explaining something you have learned recently in school.

2. Write an informal letter to a grandparent explaining something you have learned recently outside of school.

3. Write an informal thank-you letter to a friend for something (s)he did recently that made you feel good.

4. Write an informal letter to a special guest who came to your classroom to share something interesting. Thank the special guest and write something about what you learned from him/her.

5. Write an informal letter to someone in which you introduce a member of your family by writing about all his/her good points.

6. Write an informal letter to your last year's teacher and thank him/her for helping you learn enough to be a successful student this year.

7. Write an informal letter to your teacher this year and thank him/her for a recent lesson from which you learned a great deal or which made something you didn't understand more clear.

8. Write an informal letter to someone in your neighborhood and share something good that is going on at your school.

©ECS Learning Systems, Inc., San Antonio, TX

Across the Curriculum

The main application of informal letter writing across the curriculum is the students' construction of their own learning. It is important for science teachers, for instance, to teach Newton's theories of motion carefully and in the context of student involvement.

Students can picture a pool table and a cue ball hitting another ball. With at least an initial knowledge of force and momentum, they can draw conclusions on the basis of the relationship between their projections and observations. However, only if students *explain* what they think they have discovered will they overtly display what they have constructed about the physics of motion. Moreover, the explanation itself is a large part of the knowledge construction process.

In a science lesson on inertia, pairs of students might talk with one another about their observations, what they mean, and cooperatively write a sentence or two expressing the principle of inertia on their terms. These written pieces can then be "mailed" to other pairs in the room or to pen pals in other rooms for reading and comment.

English Language Learners

If understanding is the focus, students must construct basic principles in the language in which they think. The movement from informal playground talk to formal classroom language for non-native English-speaking students is based largely on what they understand and practice talking and writing about. When they write for each other, reading also becomes part of the mix.

Imagine a lesson in which pairs of students each have a wastebasket and the direction to measure the circumference and diameter with adding machine tape. By comparing the lengths of tape, they can estimate how many diameter strips could make up a circumference strip. Over time, students can go through the same process with soft drink cups, the circular clock on the wall, their circular wrist watches, the cover on the circular fan in the front of the room, etc.

Their conversation in English or in their non-English native language may focus on the following question: What does that *factor of three* mean about circles? They don't have to talk or write about *pi*, of course, but many will construct the basic knowledge that the distance around a circle is three times the distance across. They can then exchange their explanations of how circles work and send their explanations to other pairs in the room or to pen pals in another classroom.

Language Activity Sheet
Writing Informal Letters

October 12, 20xx

Dear Marco,

We are learning about how things move when they are hit. We would hit a tennis ball with another one and it would make the one we hit go off sideways. It was really neat. You should try it sometime. Maybe when I come to your house next week I can show you.

Sincerely yours,

Gerardo

1. Write the name of your partner in the science lesson. —————————————

2. Write the topic of the science lesson.————————————————

3. Write the date today.————————————————————

You are going to write a letter to your partner about what the science lesson meant, what you learned from the science lesson. The sample letter is for you to follow. Don't write what is in the sample, but follow that form for your own letter.

(Date)

(Greeting)

(Body or Message)

(Goodbye)

(Signature)

16 Power Writing

—Fluency is fundamental to the planning, or prewriting, and drafting functions of interactive writing process.

 ## Information for the Teacher

Power Writing, as a developmental writing activity, has always been about quantity first, and then quality. In this case, fluency means the ability to "get black on white," the interactive relationship between thinking about writing and the draft itself. It follows that the more automatic the draft, the more fluent the drafter, and the higher the probability that thinking about revision will occur while the draft processed.

We all want young writers to master the revision and editing function in writing, but they are thwarted by an obvious reality; they don't know what revision means. To rewrite, or revise, they often simply make their writing more legible and correct spelling errors.

Power Writing produces very rough drafts which young writers will revise. There are several important basic notions for this activity:

- The overriding purpose is quantity, and that means speed. When you direct students to begin writing, start the clock.

- Don't explain anything more than twice. Give the direction, explain it, and start. Nothing in the activity lasts long enough for anyone to be frustrated very long.

- This can be a frustrating activity on the first day, but only on the first day, and usually only for the first round of the activity. Once they figure it out, students will focus their attention on the fluency point.

- Maintain the focus: Go! Go! Go!

 ## Objective

Young writers will extend writing fluency by a factor of 20 percent between the first sample and midyear, and by another 20 percent between midyear and year's end. In addition, young writers will engage actively in revision and editing functions.

Conducting the Lesson

1. **Write on the board two words everyone will know and understand.** Direct students to select one and use it as the idea for writing in Round One. Instruct them to write as much as they can, as well as they can in one minute.

Tip

There seems to be some sort of physiological connection between the sound of a stopwatch stem being pressed down and an uncontrollable surge in focused behavior. At this sound, nearly everyone in the room will begin to write. Hold up your stop watch so they will know that you know how long one minute is. If you have to use the sweep second hand on the clock, make sure you use the one-minute criterion precisely.

Example: "Does everyone understand? I will put two words on the board, select one and use that idea as your topic for writing as much as you can as well as you can in one minute. Here we go." [Write *pony* and *mountain* on the board.] "Pick a word." [Pause perhaps five seconds, then say, "Go!," and hit the button on the stop watch.]

2. **In one minute, call time and ask the students to count the number of words they wrote.**

Example: "Time! Put your pencils down. Count your words. Count every word you wrote between when I said 'Go!' and when I said 'Time!' Put the number in a circle right above what you just wrote."

Cue

Write as much as you can as well as you can....

Get Writing!! Book 2 Grades 2-3 ©ECS Learning Systems, Inc., San Antonio, TX 139

Power Writing

3. **Make the following chart on the board, ask for a show of hands for word counts at each level, and enter them on the chart.** (**Note:** The chart below is for recording power writing from a two-word prompt. Starting here will ensure movement up the scale. In time you can move to five-word increments.) In the second grade, the word counts will likely range between 0-2 and 24-26 on the chart. In the third grade, it will top out at about 27-30.

	Round One	Round Two	Round Three
30+			
27-29			
24-26			
21-23			
18-20			
15-17			
12-14			
9-11			
6- 8			
3- 5			
0- 2			

4. **For Round Two, write two more words on the board.** Ask the students to pick one and use it as the topic for more Power Writing. Again, give them only one minute. Proceed as described in steps 1, 2, and 3.

5. **For Round Three, repeat the procedure.** The trend through the three rounds will show the average student in the room is writing approximately 20 words per minute, unprepared, on a dictated topic. Remember, the point is fluency—getting black on white. Quality will come later.

6. **Introduce the idea of revision to the class.** Give students the opportunity to choose their writing from either round. Tell them to select one and revise it so they can turn it in for a grade. Give them twice the time it took to write the draft—two minutes—and time them. Don't explain further. Ask for volunteers to tell the class how they revised their writing.

Tip

A few students will not begin writing because they don't understand the idea of revision. Tell them this is a chance to make their writing better, but if they can't think of anything to do, just sit quietly for the next minute or so.

©ECS Learning Systems, Inc., San Antonio, TX

Example: "What did you do to your writing?" (I corrected spelling and made another sentence because I didn't get a chance to finish it.) Begin a list on the board. Write *spelling* and write *new ending* on the list. "What else did you do?" (Fixed a sentence.) "How did you fix it?" (It wasn't right, so I had to write it again. It didn't make sense.) "Patrick?" (I put more in to show what it is about. It didn't have any start in it.)

7. **When the list is at least 10 items long, stop and call students' attention to it.** Tell the class this is what it means to edit and revise their work. An ongoing list of their self-reported revision and editing skills can be displayed on a bulletin board and referred to throughout the year.

   Example: "Class, look at our list of revision and editing skills. These are some of what we do when we revise and edit our writing. When I ask you to revise your work, look for sentences that don't work very well, then use the list to rewrite them more clearly."

8. **Conduct Power Writing about twice a week for a week or two, then perhaps two or three times each month thereafter.** Do the revision portion of the activity every other time. Students need the experience of revising their drafts. Knowing the revision part of the activity is in the wings makes them pay subliminal attention to quality as they produce the quantity.

Tip

Remember, the direction is always worded the same: **Write as much as you can as well as you can.**

Get Writing!! Book 2 Grades 2-3   ©ECS Learning Systems, Inc., San Antonio, TX   141

 Daily Writing Activities

Having participated in **Power Writing** once, most young writers will want to do it every day if they can get away with it. It is fun because it demonstrates achievement. Children don't compete with one another for scores because the exercise moves too quickly for them to pay attention to anything other than their own totals. They find out that they can produce lots of language on the spot. The writing they produce is a real draft to be edited and revised.

The procedures and direction are always the same. Only the idea words change. They can come from the spelling list, the literature read yesterday, or from the vocabulary list. They can come from content area reading or they can be randomly selected from a list.

roof	cabin	energy	liquid
solid	age	apple	gift
catch	desk	valley	chalk
trail	paper	napkin	salt
rug	gear	place	spill
ring	clip	goat	twist

©ECS Learning Systems, Inc., San Antonio, TX

 ## Across the Curriculum

A ready source for **Power Writing** is content-area vocabulary; the ideas that come from what students read and talk about in history, mathematics, science, and music.

In the second grade, a session from social studies might focus on community helpers such as a police officer, mail carrier, fire fighter, and so forth. A vocabulary lesson based on the notion that children learn words because of the synonyms and antonyms associated with them may yield words associated, for example, with *cold: hot, warm, tepid, luke warm, freezing, frigid, boiling*, and so forth.

Remember, the focus here is getting black on white. The words only provide a way for them to begin. They represent idea clips, that's all. However, if we can get third-graders to write freely about the words they are trying to master in their content work, all the better. Just be sure not to use the words as object lessons. The object lesson here is fluency, not vocabulary, or concepts in science.

 ©ECS Learning Systems, Inc., San Antonio, TX

English Language Learners

This lesson provides young writers whose native language is not English with an opportunity to write freely on their own terms (Power Writing) and receive reinforcement (the fluency chart) for their productivity alone. They then have an opportunity to go back and adjust what they wrote.

With some input from the children, their parents, a teacher aide, etc., corresponding word lists can represent every language in the classroom. This way, everyone has access to any list.

On occasion, add to revision the task of translating into English (perhaps by pairing students with English speakers). This activity provides leeway for young writers to produce language on their own terms. It increases comprehensibility and reduces the affective filter that produces so much avoidance of writing. In short, they can relax and just write.

　　©ECS Learning Systems, Inc., San Antonio, TX

My Own Power Writing Chart

Date	Idea Word	Round One	Round Two	Round Three

Appendix
Organizing for Long-Term Instruction

Teaching writing is about ensuring that students become better writers by learning something every day about writing well, and then practicing what they learn. The only way to ensure that this happens is to teach attributes of good writing every day. There are attributes of good writing addressed throughout the **Get Writing!!** series. They include:

- Thinking and writing in sentences and understanding the relationships between and among main ideas in sentences
- Thinking and writing in larger main ideas and understanding the relationships between and among main sentences
- Understanding the role of main ideas in paragraphs
- Thinking and writing in a variety of genres
- Progressively mastering the discipline of conventional writing

Organizing for long-term instruction is based on these factors:

1. **Mission Statement** (see below): Create a mission statement for the year. The mission statement must be about the students' writing performance and should be shared with the students. The mission statement articulates what students will be able to do by the end of the year and how that will be measured and reported. The mission statement must involve everyone in the room and include all students, individually and collectively. It is not limited to the average child in the room.

2. **Assessment** (pp. 147-152): The teacher needs a way or ways to assess and measure writing behaviors that address the mission statement.

3. **Reporting** (pp. 150): The teacher needs a way to report individual achievement of the mission statement to individual students, parents, administrators, and members of the district's governing board.

4. **Planning** (pp. 153-156): To ensure achievement of the mission, the teacher must know what both the teacher and the students will do each month, week, and day.

Sample Mission Statement

Students will be able to develop ideas and use procedures appropriate for using paragraphs to organize main ideas into short descriptions and directions, oral and written reports, and stories with dialogue. They will write in sufficient quantity* every school day to include the genres above in response to their reading, daily journal reflections, and writing across the curriculum. The quality of student writing will increase as measured by sentence maturity, control over the conventions of standard English writing, as well as clarity and organization.

* To ensure sufficient quantity, establish a daily general word-count criterion. For example it is reasonable to expect students to write as much as 300-450 words per day, or four to five pages. Set the baseline expectation at three pages of accumulated writing for the first two months of the year, and increase it to five pages by the end of the year. Most of the writing is practice. It must be monitored, but it does not have to be read, graded, noted with marginal messages, and sent home to be signed.

The emphasis here is on the teacher. The teacher must forge a *systematic* writing instruction program in his/her classroom without a systematic instructional program the children's writing won't be appreciably better at the end of the year than it was at the beginning.

Assessment in the Balanced Writing Program

Assessment is an integral part of all fundamental teaching. In reading assessment, we all essentially agree to look for word attack and comprehension. In mathematics assessment, we all essentially agree that we should observe numeration, operations, measurement, probability, statistics, and problem solving. But in writing, you may not agree with our ideas for assessment and we may not agree with yours. Likewise, the National Council of Teachers of English may not agree with the ideas of the *New York Times* or the Midwest Committee on Workplace Literacy, if there is such a group.

There is a serious implication here: *If no one agrees, there is no formal, relatively uniform assessment frame of reference, no relatively uniform assessment schedule or process.* The result? We all teach to whatever we determine should be the tests of writing quality, which can mean anything anyone decides it should mean. And if quality can mean anything, in practical application, it means nothing.

What is Quality Writing?

List what you look for and how you assess student writing. There are only seven spaces below. That doesn't mean there are only seven items. If you need more space, continue writing on a separate sheet.

1.

2.

3.

4.

5.

6.

7.

Appendix
Assessment

 ### The Scoring System

The following list includes three items which we (your authors) look for in student writing samples. Understand however, that these are not the only measure of writing ability.

1. **Fluency,** or *How much did the child write?* Fluency can be measured by counting the words the student wrote in a specified amount of time (**x** words in **y** minutes). Fluency is not a measure of writing quality, but it's important to recognize that without fluency, a writer's chance of producing quality writing is severely compromised.

2. **Maturity,** or *What is the syntactic sophistication of the sentences the child wrote?* Maturity can be measured by dividing the number of words the child wrote by the number of sentences. We can measure maturity by counting the clauses in the writing sample and dividing the number of clauses by the number of sentences. Complexity is not, by itself, a measure of quality in writing. But as young writers develop, their ideas get more sophisticated, and they need more sophisticated and complex ways to structure their ideas in writing.

3. **Mechanical Control,** or *To what extent does the writing sample display the structure and discipline that makes written language work?* Mechanical control can be measured by counting errors in capitalization, punctuation, spelling, usage, and sentence construction. We can then total the errors and divide the total by the number of sentences.

 ### Questions and Answers

Look over the items on your list (p. 147) and on our list. Then ask yourself the following questions:

1. *Does each item lead directly and predictably to the ability to write well?*

2. *To what extent can you measure—not evaluate or judge, but quantify—the items on your lists so you can assess them again and chart progress after several weeks of instruction?*

Here are our answers to these two questions:

1. No one learns to write well without writing something. Our three assessment items lead directly and predictably to writing well because they cause the child to write something. The quality of writing is carried, to a large extent, in sentence maturity appropriate to audience and purpose. As children mature, their audience tends to mature, and their purpose tends to get more sophisticated.

2. Communication in writing depends on readers; and readers can understand what is being communicated, to a large extent, because writers make print follow certain capitalization, punctuation, spelling, usage, and sentence patterns. Thus, writing is called "good," to some extent, because it is mechanically accurate.

Each of our assessment items can be counted, thus quantified and measured again. A second assessment will show what the children learned on the three measures of writing ability.

As the writers of this book, we cannot specify what your assessment variables should be. We can, however, recommend different ways to look at assessment, such as the following, based on the analytic criteria: **fluency, maturity,** and **mechanical control.**

The First Monday Assessment

On the first Monday of the year, collect a writing sample for analytic assessment. Direct students to write a journal entry about something they learned recently, something they did that made them feel good, something they taught someone else to do, something they know how to do. Focus on this type of topic—children are experts on themselves.

Students will often ask if spelling counts. Tell them that spelling always counts: "Spell as well as you can all the time, but don't stop writing just because you don't know how to spell a word. If you come to a word you think you don't know how to spell, use enough of the right letters so you'll be able to read it later, and then make it right."

If students ask about punctuation, tell them it always counts and to always write as well as they can. Tell them also that if they come to a place where they are not sure what to do, to try their best, then make a mark at the end of the line and go back to it later and make it right. But to never stop writing just because they don't know what punctuation mark to use.

 ## The Writing Sample

Prepare students for assessment by making sure they have paper and pencil or pen. If your students use word processors, set them up, individually, at a keyboard and screen. Tell them that you will give them the topic, and they will write "as much as they can as well as they can." Then prompt a writing sample, getting them to think by giving them oral suggestions. **Note:** This is all oral on the teacher's part and mental on the childrens'.

Example: Mentally take them into their home. On this imaginary tour, they walk around the house and feel what it's like to be there. They look into all the rooms. They choose one room, any room, and go inside. They look around. Direct them to think about why they chose that room.

Ask them to think about what's in the room, who tends to be there, what is done there. Ask them to think about all the things they know about that room. Say, "Boys and girls, I want you to write about that room in your house. You may write in whatever way you wish, but you are to write as much as you can as well as you can. You have five minutes. [Pause a count or two.] Begin."

Nearly every child will begin to write at this prompt. The few who raise their hand for clarification can be answered simply with the direction, "Do you have a room? Choose a room in your house. Write about that room." If the child tells you that (s)he can't think of anything, simply encourage.

Tip

If a child writes nothing, that's the score for this initial assessment. This isn't unfair. If you're assessing reading and the child doesn't read, there is nothing to assess, so you wait for the next time. No effort, no behavior, or no production, is an assessment. Don't be concerned. It's the rare child who writes nothing, and we've never seen it happen twice.

Appendix
Assessment

 ## The First Week Assessment

During the first week of school, collect one more writing sample. For these first-week writing samples, give students only five minutes to write. Make sure every student has the same amount of time to write.

After collecting the first writing sample and having the children count the words, play a little sentence-writing game for a few minutes. The children enjoy it, it feels like a puzzle, and children get a sense of their own control by doing it.

"Think of a sentence that contains a weather word." (**It's raining outside, and I'm getting wet**.) After students have generated several sentences and shared them aloud, change the cue.

"Think of a five-word sentence that contains a weather word." (**Rain is good for plants**.)

Each sentence must have exactly five words. Listen to several sentences and change the cue again.

"This time, think of a five-word sentence in which a weather word is in the third position." (**It was snowing on Saturday**.)

After students generate several sentences aloud, have them write one on their paper as a Ticket to Recess. During the recess break, read their sentences and post them on the Best Effort Board. When students return from recess, direct their attention to a Best Effort Board and tell them there will be best efforts every day this year. They will be responsible for choosing and posting their best effort each day. Tell students, *"We never post anything that isn't our best effort. You must decide what your best effort is. Oh, and we will write every day so there will be best efforts each day."*

 ## Follow-Up Assessment

To determine whether the objectives related to fluency and mechanical control have been satisfied or at least approached, the teacher might conduct a five-minute writing sample on Friday of the second week.

 ## Scoring the Sample and Reporting

When students finish their writing sample, direct them to count the words they wrote and put the number in a circle at the top of their paper. When they have finished counting, direct them to count again for the sake of accuracy and put the number in another circle at the top of the page. Then collect the papers.

Using the scoring system explained below, determine the scores for each writing sample and record the results on the assessment form (p. 152), one set of scores per sheet. Conducting two writing samples takes into account that children have good days and not-so-good days. They also write better to some cues or situations than others. By writing two times under two circumstances, the average of the week's samples is a better gauge of how the children write than a single sample.

Important Note: A total of two to three hours for analytic assessment to identify baseline performance, establish instructional objectives, and show the magnitude of progress isn't unbearable—especially since this data can show the parents, the principal, the school board, and

©ECS Learning Systems, Inc., San Antonio, TX

the local newspaper about how children are, in fact, learning to write quite well. Before you throw your hands up and say there isn't time in your day to do what we're suggesting here, remember that the time consumed in most assessment processes is vastly "front-loaded." If it takes an hour to do running records on ten children, the first four children consume 30 minutes, and the other six are done in the last 30 minutes. We get better with practice.

With practice, this analytic assessment system takes between 30 and 50 seconds to complete for each child. After scoring about six children, a teacher can complete each one in under one minute. That's about 30 to 40 minutes for the class. Two samples in the first week demands about 70 to 90 minutes. There will be another analytic assessment about midyear, and then again at the end of the year, with only one sample each time.

 ## *First Week Analytic Assessment: A Class Scenario*

The following are very plausible average figures for a second-grade's first week of analytic assessment:

# Words:	**14**
# Sentences:	**3**
# Clauses:	**3**
Word/Snt:	**4.66**
Clauses/Snt:	**1.0**
Total Errors:	**7**
Errors/Snt:	**2.33**

In five minutes, this class writes an average of 14 words in an average of 3 essentially simple sentences. The average number of words per sentence is 5; the average number of clauses per sentence is 1. On the average, there are 7 errors per sample, or 2.3 per average sentence. Of course, there are children in the room who write more words, some who write an error-free draft, some who write compound, even complex sentences. Others will write fewer words and commit many errors. But the averages are those that appear above.

Based on these averages, the teacher establishes two objectives for the following two months:
1. Increase number of words per sentence to 20 or more
2. Decrease error rate to 1.5 or less

On Monday of the following week, the teacher might focus on Objective 16 in Book 2 (extend fluency 20% in first half year and 20% more in second half year). To that end, the teacher conducts Power Writing on Monday, Wednesday, and Thursday of the week and uses the revision portion of Power Writing on both Wednesday and Thursday. The teacher might also focus on Objectives 2, 4, and 5 (sentence writing, capital letters at the beginning of sentences, and end marks at the end of sentences). The teacher plans at least ten minutes of both oral and written attention to each of the three objectives (2, 4, and 5) on Monday, Tuesday, Wednesday, and Thursday. In addition, the teacher plans for students to write at least two autobiographical pieces between Monday and Friday (see Objective 4, Book 2).

Friday Follow-Up Assessment: To determine whether the objectives related to fluency and mechanical control have been satisfied or at least approached, the teacher might conduct a five-minute writing sample on Friday of the second week.

Writing Assessment Worksheet

Date: _____

Student Names	#Words	#Sentences	#Clauses	#Words/ Sentences	Clauses/ Sentences	Cp	Pn	Sp	SNT Errors*	E/S
_____										_____
_____										_____
_____										_____
_____										_____
_____										_____
_____										_____
_____										_____
_____										_____
_____										_____
_____										_____
_____										_____
_____										_____
_____										_____
_____										_____
_____										_____
_____										_____
_____										_____
_____										_____

Averages**_____

*Cp: Capitalization errors
Pn: Punctuation Errors
Sp: Spelling Errors
SNT: Sentence Structure Errors (Fragments, Run-ons, and Usage)
E/S: Total Errors divided by Number of Sentences Equals Errors per Sentence (E/S)

** Totals divided by number of writing samples provides a baseline for establishing a two- or three-month objective. (For example, if the the average number of words is 32, the objective may be to increase the class average by 10% in two months, 10% more in next two months, and 10% more by the end of the year.

Sample Instruction Plans

 ## One-Year Writing Instruction Plan

The prototype one-year plan for third grade on pages 154-155 begins with specification of genre study by the month. When a specific genre is identified for a month (September - Fiction), the elements of short story are taught and written during that month. This does not mean that September will be a month when the children merely write stories. It does mean students will write stories based on a study of story grammar (character, setting, problem, resolution) and elements (dialogue to reveal character, brevity, coherence, focus, and so forth). Such fiction study and writing appears in Objectives 5, 6, 7, 8, 9, and 13 in Book 2.

 ## One-Month Writing Instruction Plan

A one-month instructional plan for September appears on page 156. Look at Monday of Week I. You will see the following entry: "Set up Interactive Journal #15." The Interactive Journal is a genre (Book 2); #15 corresponds to Objective 15 in Book 2's list of Objectives. On Tuesday of Week I, the second line (Sentences #1) corresponds to Objective 1 in Book 1.

You should notice several things in this one-month sample plan.

- There is both direct instruction and independent writing every day.
- There is more than one audience for every third-grader's writing.
- Students work both with genres and with craft throughout the month
- There is an assessment target for the month (fluency).
- The students will write as many as 5 stories and 13 story starts.

Given the one-year plan and one-month sample plan, you can personalize each month of writing instruction according to the one-year plan in this book, or according to a personal variation on what appears in the one-year plan.

Remember: Students must write in great quantity. They must be better writers at the end of the month than they were at the beginning *because* of what they learned from their teacher and each other and practiced on their own.

Sample One-Year Writing Calendar

Month	Genres	Construction	Mechanical Control
September	• Fiction • Interactive Journal with fifth- or sixth-grade partner • Poem-a-Day	• Single sentence writing • Power Writing (w/weekly revision)	• Review of punctuation and capitalization conventions
October	• Report of Information • Each child has at least one story in process at all times; must submit at least one in Oct. • Interactive Journal • Poem-a-Day	• Single/Double sentence thinking and writing • Power Writing with revision	• Comma in compound and complex sentences • Comma to separate items in series
November	• Autobiographical Incident (three each week) • Collaborative Report of Information in Social Studies • Interactive Journal • Poem-a-Day	• Single/Double/Triple sentence thinking and writing • Power Writing with revision (twice in November)	• Reinforce prior conventions • Apostrophe in contractions
December	• Autobiographical Incident (weekly) • Reader Response to reading • Interactive Journal • Poem-a-Day	• Sentences to Paragraphs • Power Writing with revision (twice in December)	• Reinforce student responsibility for mechanical control
January	• Autobiographical Incident (weekly) • Reader Response to reading • Interactive Journal • Poem-a-Day	• Paragraph-a-Day • Power Writing with revision (twice in January)	• Apostrophe in singular possessive—if it appeares in student writing

Month			
February	• Formal Letters • Informal Letters • Reader Response to reading • Autobiographical Incident (weekly) • Fiction option • Poem-a-Day	• Two- and three-paragraph writings for transitions • Power Writing with revision (once in February)	• Pronouns as transitional devices • Responsibility for all prior conventions
March	• Opinion Essay • Formal Letter to the opinion editor of the local newspaper • Autobiographical Incident (weekly) • Choice: Reader Response, Informal Letter, Fiction • Poem-a-Day	• Sentence Combining • Power Writing with revision (once in March)	• Writing with nouns and verbs
April	• Opinion Essay • Student Choice • Poem-a-Day	• Sentence Combining Power Writing with revision (once in April)	• Writing with nouns, verbs, adjectives, adverbs
May	• Student Choice • Poem-a-Day	• Review all sentence and paragraph activities	• Writing with nouns, verbs, adjectives, adverbs
June	• Final organization and preparation of of portfolio for Literacy Faire		• Application of all conventions to final revision of materials for Literacy Faire

Sample One-Month Calendar
September

	Monday	Tuesday	Wednesday	Thursday	Friday
Week One	• Writing Sample • Read a Poem • Set up Interactive Journal #15	• Fiction: Character #6 • Sentences #1 • Read a Poem • Capitalization (Cp) Review	• Fiction: Character #6 • Read a Poem • Punctuation (Pn) Review • Power Writing #16	• Fiction: Dialogue • Sentences #2 • Read a Poem	• Fiction: Use dialogue to reveal character in story #13 • Sentence Writing #2 • Third-graders meet with fifth- or sixth-grade partners
Week Two	• Common Story #8 • Journals to Olders • Read a Poem • Sentences #4 • Cp/Pn Reinforce	• Dialogue for Monday's Common Story #13 • Read a Poem • Sentences #4 • Power Writing #16	• Finish Common Story • Journals from Olders • Read a Poem • Sentences #4	• New Common Story #8 • Journals to Olders • Read a Poem • Sentences #4 • Cp/Pn Reinforce	• Finish Common Story #8 • Sentences #2 or #4 • Read a Poem
Week Three	• Setting • Description #9 • Read a Poem • Journal from Olders Power Writing #16	• Describe another Story Setting #9 • Read a Poem • Sentences #2	• Write a character into Monday's or Tuesday's Setting #6 and #9 • Read a Poem Journal to Olders Sentences #2	• Continue Story from Wednesday • Read a Poem • Sentences #2 or #4	• Finish story • Read a Poem • Journal from Olders • Sentences #2 or #4
Week Four	• Start a Story with a Character #6 • Journal to Olders • Sentences #2 or 4	• Start a Story with a Setting #7 • Read a Poem • Cp final review	• Outline Common Story #8 • Journal from Olders • Power Writing #16	• Fiction from one of three Story Starts • Sentences #2 or #4 • Pn. final review	• Writing Sample: Score for fluency • Continue Thursday story with emphasis on dialogue

©ECS Learning Systems, Inc., San Antonio, TX

Bibliography

Farnan, N., D. Rocha-Hill, and L. Fearn. (1994). *We Can All Write*. San Diego: Kabyn Books.

Farnan, N., E. Goldman, and L. Fearn. (1985). *Developing Writers in Grades 7 - 12*. San Diego: Kabyn Books.

Farnan, N. and L. Fearn. (1994). "The Writing Program in Action: A Writer's Ruminations about Portfolios," *Writing Teacher*, VII, May, 26-27.

Fearn, L. (1976). "Individual Development: A Process Model in Creativity," *Journal of Creative Behavior*, 10 , 55-64.

_____. (1981). *(The First) First I Think*. San Diego: Kabyn Books.

_____. (1981). "Teaching Writing by Teaching Thinking." *Academic Therapy*, 17:173-178

Fearn, L. and K. Foster. (1979). *The Writing Kabyn*. San Diego: Kabyn Books.

Prior, J. A. (1979). "The Impact of Developmental Writing Instruction on Learning Handicapped Students." Unpublished Masters Degree Thesis, San Diego: San Diego State University.

Notes

Notes

Notes

Get Writing!! Book 2 Grades 2-3 ©ECS Learning Systems, Inc., San Antonio, TX